FATHER J.-P. DE CAUSSADE, S.J.

Self-Abandonment to Divine Providence

TRANSLATED FROM THE
STANDARD FRENCH EDITION OF
FATHER P. H. RAMIÈRE, S.J.
BY
Algar Thorold

REVISED BY
Father John Joyce, S.J.

WITH AN INTRODUCTION BY
David Knowles
Emeritus Professor of Modern History
in the University of Cambridge

COLLINS
THE FONTANA LIBRARY OF
THEOLOGY AND PHILOSOPHY

This translation, first published by Burns & Oates Ltd in 1933,
was revised by Father John Joyce, S.J., in 1959
First issued in the Fontana Library of Theology and Philosophy, 1971

Made and Printed in Great Britain by
William Collins Sons & Co Ltd Glasgow

NIHIL OBSTAT: ADRIANVS VAN VLIET, S.T.D.
CENSOR DEPVTATVS
IMPRIMATVR: E. MORROGH BERNARD
VICARIVS GENERALIS
WESTMONASTERII: DIE XIV FEBRVARII MCMLIX

CONTENTS

INTRODUCTION

By David Knowles

The treatise on Self-abandonment is a spiritual classic of the first order. It was a mannerism of Lord Macaulay to erect in every department of history and letters a hierarchy of excellence—the half-dozen greatest Athenians, the five greatest epic poems, and so forth—a poor substitute, so his detractors say, for true criticism. We all do the like at times, I imagine, and if we set ourselves to choose the ten greatest spiritual guides since St Bernard—a magnificent list, indeed, including St Teresa, St John of the Cross and St Francis de Sales—it would without a doubt be necessary to find a place for Père de Caussade. Certainly few apart from the saints have received such unstinted praise from all parts of the Church of today. In France two of the judges best qualified to speak, Père Garrigou-Lagrange and M. Henri Bremond, have repeatedly spoken of him in terms of reverent admiration. A still greater testimony, as well to the depth and sureness of his teaching as to his value as a living, helping force, is experience itself. How many souls, both in France and (though in smaller numbers) in this country, have found in Caussade their greatest stay—perhaps their only resource—at a particular period of their spiritual life. How many others have found, not this, but—sure token of a classic—a steady friendship to which they can return again and again, not at a period of crisis but during the ordinary flow of life. *L'Abandon* then is a book for all those who, in St Benedict's words, truly seek God. It has been translated and printed not to be explained or to be criticized, but to be read, and for the majority of readers of the kind Caussade would have desired, no introduction is necessary.

Yet since he is still an unknown figure to many Englishmen; since to some who read widely he is bound to challenge comparison with others; since, in fine, despite his discursive exterior he has a clearly defined doctrine for us to learn, there seems room for a word of introduction which endeavours to give, in his own words, the main lines of his teaching, and to indicate what masters he himself appears to have been willing to follow.

I. Very little is known of the life of Caussade, and since Abbot Chapman has set out this little in an article in the *Dublin Review* in January 1931 (which also appeared as an introduction to Caussade's dialogues *On Prayer*),[1] we may pass at once to consider his spiritual teaching. It has come down to us in three books: *L'Abandon*; the above-mentioned treatise in the form of dialogues on prayer; and a considerable number of letters to a small group of correspondents, almost all religious of the Visitation. The treatise and the letters, although they throw very valuable light on Caussade's mind, do not add in any essentials to the teaching of *L'Abandon*, which, as in form it is undoubtedly his masterpiece, so in matter is the very kernel of his doctrine.

Père de Caussade's spiritual teaching was derived from two extremely pure sources, St Francis de Sales and St John of the Cross. That he should be beholden to St Francis was only to have been expected. Bremond has shown us how deep was St Francis's influence on French religious thought in the century that followed his death, and Caussade received this influence from at least two different directions. We know from his own words how great was the influence of Bossuet upon him.

[1] See also Biographical Note, p. 26 below.

Bossuet, though by no means wholly Salesian, knew St Francis well and took from him a number of leading ideas. Several of these, and above all abandonment to divine Providence and confidence in God, are precisely those which most attract Caussade. But another source of influence was probably still more potent. Caussade, like all directors, must have learnt much from his penitents, and these were, for the most part, nuns of the Visitation. He would naturally wish to express himself in an idiom with which they were familiar and steep himself in the writings of their law-giver, and we are not surprised to find many traces of resemblance, both doctrinal and verbal, between him and St Francis.[1] Indeed, the two phrases which recur most frequently in his treatises and letters—abandonment to divine Providence and the value of the present moment—are peculiarly Salesian, and it is noteworthy that whereas the Carmelite school, following St Teresa and St John, when speaking of the death to self use by choice the evangelical words 'poverty', 'renunciation' and 'death', Caussade instinctively turns to 'abandonment', 'trust' and 'acquiescence'. Yet in speaking of Salesian influence we must make a distinction. The mode of expression, as is well known, if not the whole method, of St Francis underwent a remarkable development as the result of his experience with the Visitation at Annecy, and in particular with the way of helplessness and desolation by which St Jane Frances was led. The deepest and most intimate chapters of *The Love of God* are of an entirely different colour—one had almost said, of an entirely different culture—from the *Introduction*, the early letters and even some of the *Conferences*. It is to this

[1] Cf. *The Love of God*, viii, 3-7, 14; ix, 1-6, 15; *Conferences*, ii, xv. I owe these references to Père Garrigou-Lagrange, O.P., *La Providence* (Desclée, 1932), p. 231. See also Bossuet, *Etats d'oraison*, viii. 9.

later period, the Visitandine, Chantal period, that Caussade is related, and the tone of *L'Abandon* is in many places almost precisely that of the deepest chapters of *The Love of God*.

The second great source of Caussade's doctrine is the school of Carmel, and especially St John of the Cross. During his maturity the long-dormant interest of the Church as a whole had been reawakened by St John's canonization in 1726. In Spain a serious attempt was made to print a critical edition of his works, and in any case his doctrine was now placed beyond the breath of calumny. There are specific references to him in the dialogues on prayer, but one does not get the impression that Caussade used him as a guiding textbook, and I am not aware that Caussade was thrown often into direct contact with Carmelites. Nevertheless, his mystical theology, as we shall see, squares exactly with the scheme set out in the *Ascent* and the *Dark Night* and treated as classic by the Carmelite theologians. This agreement is all the more remarkable because it is implicit rather than explicit. Caussade does not, of preference, throw the same aspects or moments of the spiritual life into high light; his compositions are not in the same key as St John's; he has not that peculiar Carmelite family likeness which Anne of Jesus, let us say, shares both with St John and with St Teresa of Lisieux. Yet I think there can be no doubt that his doctrine, as formulated in *L'Abandon*, can be equated with St John's far more fully than can St Francis's or Père Grou's. Perhaps equation is not the best term; Caussade's achievement is rather one of synthesis. He, and he alone of the great French spiritual writers, superimposes on the Salesian teaching of self-abandonment and simplicity the typically Carmelite emphasis on grace as a dynamic force, enlightening and cleansing the soul.

We look, and, so far as I am aware, we look in vain,

for another source of influence on Caussade. Within his own Society, and in France, there had been a succession of eminent directors who drew their inspiration from the great Lallemant. Caussade cannot, one would think, have been unaware of this tradition or unsympathetic to it. His outlook is, in fact, very close to that of the Lallemant school, and not at all close to that of Rodriguez and Bourdaloue. Yet so far as I have noticed he makes no direct reference to Lallemant; certainly there is in *L'Abandon* no trace of emphasis on the points so dear to Lallemant himself—the sharp opposition of active and contemplative, the exposition of the gifts of the Holy Ghost, the insistence on the need for a 'second conversion'.

We may now look a little more closely at the leading ideas of Caussade's teaching, and the whole system into which they fit. Chief amongst them is, of course, the one which gives its title to the present treatise—the word Caussade has made peculiarly his own—*L'Abandon*.[1] The translator has decided to render this by the compound English word 'self-abandonment'. This is probably as near as our language can get to the French word, but his readers must ultimately learn from Caussade's whole body of teaching the full meaning of the term. For the moment, it is important to remember that 'self-abandonment' does not for him directly signify the active, ascetic renunciation of self, self-love and self-wit. The process, rightly emphasized by all ascetical writers and occupying a very large place in Carmelite spirituality, occupies a relatively minor place in Caussade's thought, not because he neglects, but because he assumes it. His 'self-abandonment' is, in its primary

[1] In Littré's *Dictionnaire* the first quotation of *abandon* is from Bossuet, and he gives as the meaning: *remise entre les mains de*. His résumé of the growth of the word's usage is as follows: *remettre, céder, confier, laisser aller délaisser*.

sense, an acceptance of the will of God, a submission to it. On the second page of the book our Lady's *Fiat mihi* is given us as our exemplar. But the meaning of the word, as his doctrine develops, deepens still further. Two common uses of the word in English may help us to an appreciation. We speak of a swimmer abandoning himself to the waves or to the current. He may or may not wish to swim against, across or with them; in any case he finds that his independent efforts are useless or needless, and he abandons himself to the waters. We speak of one abandoning himself to grief. From this motive or that, by distraction or compulsion, with hope of success or without it, he has kept grief from mastering him. He now opens his heart to it and becomes all grief. It masters him and yet it is what his heart desires. If we substitute the divine action for the waters of the sea or of sorrow in these two phrases, we shall have a faint, inaccurate conception of the deepest meaning of Caussade's 'self-abandonment'—inaccurate because in the case of co-operation with grace the human liberty and, at least normally, the human effort is still, and must be, present.

But let us return to the root meaning of 'self-abandonment'. Acceptance of the will of God, whether signified to us by command, counsel and inspiration, or manifested by the ordinances of divine Providence, is the duty of every Christian. It is a virtue; it may be taught and practised by repeated acts. But 'self-abandonment' in Caussade's vocabulary means something more. It means the real, effective gift to God of all the powers of the soul. It means the attitude, the outlook of a soul so given. It means the state of a soul caught up, so to say, in God's machinery, for whom the supernatural life is more real than the natural. *Vivo ego, jam non ego.* Caussade's first editor, the saintly Père Ramière, S.J., tells us that the treatise, as he printed it, is a mixture of letters and conferences taken down by one of the audience. The order and divisions which we now have are Ramière's, not Caussade's. His aim was to divide matter which would be useful to all souls from that which would primarily be of use only to advanced souls. In the first division he tried to collect instructions for acquiring the virtue of abandonment; in the second, advice for those who were in the state of abandonment. This division serves its purpose to some extent, but it does not really correspond to any development in Caussade's thought. In his *Letters*, indeed, we see how he speaks to beginners and those not in religion, but *L'Abandon* is addressed in its entirety to souls of whom he is certain—chosen souls, contemplatives.

II. We have, then, to find in Caussade the outlines of a theory of mystical theology. Let us first hear his aim:

> *I wish to show all that they may lay claim, not to the same distinct favours, but to the same love, the same self-abandonment, the same God . . . and to eminent sanctity.*
>
> *Let us not distress or refuse anyone, or drive any away from eminent perfection. Jesus calls all to perfection. . . . If we knew how to leave God's divine hand free to act, we should attain the most eminent perfection. All would attain it, for it is offered to all.*

The last sentences show clearly enough that by perfection and sanctity Caussade means the complete perfection of a fully purified soul. Its origin is in sanctifying grace:

> *The presence of God which sanctifies our souls is that indwelling of the Holy Trinity which is established in the depths of our hearts when they submit to the divine will.*

And its end is:

To form Jesus Christ in the depth of our hearts.

We for our part have to do no more than give our whole heart really to God:

The free gift which he asks from our hearts consists of abnegation, obedience and love; the rest is God's affair.

In other words there

is but one thing to do: to purify our hearts, to detach ourselves from creatures, and abandon ourselves entirely to God,

because

The divine action . . . can only take possession of a soul in so far as it is empty of all confidence in its own action.

That is the pure doctrine of St John, as is also this:

To do all this in a holy manner, you have but to change your heart. What is meant by the heart is the will.

In the process of detachment, the purely natural activities of the reason must give way to supernatural faith:

Our understanding wishes to take the first place among the divine methods; it must be reduced to the last.

Likewise the life of the senses must go:

We must kill our senses and be stripped of them; their destruction means the reign of faith,

and faith must take their place:

Faith is what I preach, self-abandonment, confidence and faith; willingly to be the subject and instrument of divine action. . . . Faith gives the aspect of heaven to the whole earth, it is by faith that the heart is ravished, transplanted . . . faith only reaches the truth without seeing it; it touches what it does not perceive.

And so:

The life of faith is nothing but the continual pursuit

> *of God through everything that disguises, disfigures, destroys and, so to say, annihilates him.*

When we have given ourselves to God, he begins to work upon us, not by developing our natural gifts and instincts:

> *This work* (of the Holy Spirit) *is not accomplished by way of our own cleverness or intelligence, or subtlety of mind, but by way of our passive self-abandonment to its reception. . . .*

We remember St John's axiom: 'Contemplation is to receive.'[1] Caussade continues:

> *All we have to do is to receive what we are given and allow ourselves to be acted upon . . .*

for

> *God teaches the heart not by ideas, but by pains and contradictions.*

And therefore:

> *In order to reach the highest stage of perfection, the crosses sent by Providence, which are provided by their state at every moment, open to them a surer and far quicker road than extraordinary states and works.*

But this self-abasement, we must remember, is itself the work of God:

> *While he strips of everything the souls who give themselves absolutely to him, God gives them something which takes the place of all; of light, wisdom, life and force: this gift is his love,*

and love leads to a greater self-abandonment:

> (The soul) *abandoned by creatures knows only how to abandon itself and place itself in the hands of God by a love which is most real, most genuine and most active although it has been silently infused into the soul.*

The theological justification of this self-abandonment,

[1] *The Living Flame* (Baker, 1912), p. 82.

its method and its excellence, takes up a series of pages at the beginning of the treatise which both for pure beauty of style and sustained eloquence of pleading is a masterpiece of literature.

So far, in these passages which have been taken from the early pages of the book, Caussade has been insisting that abandonment of self-will and the throwing of the soul open to divine action are all in all, and that the divine action is present—and should be perceptible to the eye of faith—in every event of life, and that no single external circumstance is more than a temporary instrument of God's action which shows us God's will here and now. In what follows he proceeds to look a little more carefully at God's more intimate action. If our first task is to realize that God is in everything, the next is to realize that he is more particularly in everything that crosses the natural self:

> *The doctrine of pure love can only be learned through the action of God, and not as the result of our own activity of mind. God instructs the heart by sufferings and contradictions, not by ideas. . . .*

(We are approaching the traditional doctrine of passive purification.)

> *To possess this science, it is necessary to be disengaged from all particular goods; and, to arrive at this detachment, it is necessary to be really deprived of these goods. Thus, it is only by mortifications of all sorts, by trials and deprivations of all kinds, that we can be established in pure love. We must reach the point at which the whole of creation is nothing to us and God everything.*

The soul which began by seeing and using creatures by a purely natural light, must end by seeing and using them by a purely supernatural light, and before this can happen they must become nothing to it. Hence all created things must be reduced:

First to nothing and then to the point they have to occupy in God's Order.

This is, almost verbally, the doctrine of St Francis:

It is love which, entering into a soul to make it happily die to itself and live to God, bereaves it of all human desires. . . . Theotimus, he who has forsaken all for God ought to resume nothing but according to God's good pleasure. . . . God commanded the prophet Isaias to strip himself naked; and *he did so . . . and then the time prefixed by God having expired, he* resumed his clothes. *Even so are we to . . . die with our Saviour naked upon the cross, and rise again with him in newness of life.*[1]

This applies to all the soul's sight of itself, and of its way, aims and progress:

(God) *desires an entire handing over the soul to him. If one has the conviction that his guidance is good, one has no longer faith nor self-abandonment.*

The waters are indeed deepening; we are in the Night of the Spirit, the night of faith and hope:

Previously, the soul saw by its own ideas and lights how the plan of its perfection was working out; this is no longer the case when it is in this condition. . . . God now communicates himself to it as Life, but is no longer before its eyes as the Way and the Truth. The Bride seeks the Bridegroom in the night: he is behind her and holds her in his hands.

We are also in the night of love:

A far more grievous trial for a soul who desires nothing but to love its God, is the impossibility in which it finds itself of assuring itself that it loves him. . . .

and again:

To steal God from a heart which desires but God, what a secret of love! It is indeed a great secret of love, for by that means (and only by that means is

[1] *The Love of God*, ix, 16.

it possible) pure faith and pure hope are established in a soul,

and he gives the reason in words which St John could not better:

The more one appears to lose with God, the more one gains; the more he deprives us of the natural, the more he gives us of the supernatural. We loved him a little for his gifts; when these are no longer perceptible, we arrive at loving him for himself alone.

This summary of Caussade's teaching will have shown how traditional is his outlook and how closely he is in agreement with the great mystical theologians of the Dominican and Carmelite schools. Especially is this the case in his assumption throughout that for the growth of a soul to perfection the passive purifications are absolutely necessary, whether they take the form of ordinary or extraordinary sufferings, or whether they are part of the direct action of God on the soul, infusing purifying light. Caussade, in *L'Abandon*, is scarcely occupied at all with 'states' of prayer or a defence of contemplation. He was in fact speaking to contemplatives and therefore had no need to be. But it is possible to extract from his *obiter dicta* a perfectly consistent theory. We have seen that he equates perfection with self-abandonment and proclaims that both may be aimed at by all:

Let us teach all simple and God-fearing hearts self-abandonment to the divine action . . . let us not distress or drive away anyone from the path of eminent perfection. Jesus calls all to it.

And this perfection is the full, supernatural flower of the Christian life, disclosed in St Paul's epistles. It is the life of the saints; there is not another 'mystical' perfection beyond; this *is* mystical perfection:

All souls would arrive at supernatural, sublime, wonderful, inconceivable states of prayer. . . . Yes, if one

> *could only leave the hand of God to do its work, one would reach the most eminent perfection. All souls would reach it, for it is offered to all.*

And while he insists that for this perfection there is no need of states, works or favours which are theologically speaking 'abnormal' or 'extraordinary', since:

> *In order to reach the highest stage of perfection, the crosses sent them by Providence, with which their state of life supplies them at every moment, open to them a far surer and swifter path than extraordinary states and works,*

yet he is equally insistent that the way and grace to which he invites are *de facto* uncommon and eminent:

> *I wish to make all see that they can aim . . . at eminent sanctity. What are called extraordinary and privileged graces are so called solely because few souls are faithful enough to make themselves worthy of them.*

The careful reader of the two last extracts in their context will surely feel that the distinction between what is strictly extraordinary (the *gratiae gratis datae*, visions, the gift of prophecy and the like) and what is *de facto* extraordinary because eminent and therefore uncommon (sanctity and contemplation) has rarely been grasped more clearly or expressed more lucidly.

Indeed, the perfect agreement here as elsewhere—it is more than agreement, it is a real and pervading similarity of soul—between Caussade and St Teresa of the Infant Jesus[1] is most striking and consoling. It is well known that St Teresa took for her master St John of the Cross and was a living exemplar of his doctrine. But in the manner of her presentation of the message—in her 'secret', in her 'little way'—she reminds us far more of Caussade, whom, so far as I am aware, she had not read. No one at all familiar with the *Histoire d'une*

[1]St Thérèse of Lisieux, *The Little Flower.*

Ame can fail to note the general resemblance; it will be enough here to underline some of the distinctively personal features of the saint which are anticipated in *L'Abandon*. Her very definition of the 'little way' is in words that might be his:

> *The little way is one of spiritual childhood, of confidence and complete self-abandonment.*

Her devotion to the Infancy and Passion of our Lord, it will be remembered, did not spring, as it does with the majority of Christians, from the natural love and sympathy that childhood and suffering evoke, but from the peculiarly pure faith in the supernatural, challenged and called out, so to say, by the divinity veiled in Nazareth and still more impenetrably veiled—annihilated, in Caussade's word—in the Passion. We find the same devotion in *L'Abandon*:

> *Ask Mary, Joseph, the wise men, the shepherds: they will tell you that they find in this extreme poverty a something which renders God greater and more lovable. The deficit of the senses increases and enriches faith: the less there is for the eyes, the more for the soul. . . . The life of faith is nothing but a perpetual pursuit of God through everything that disguises, disfigures. destroys him and, if we may use the word, annihilates him.*

We think at once of the most characteristic traits of St Teresa's autobiography—of her ever-growing capacity to see, in the light of faith, the supernatural significance of apparently ordinary incidents in her own life and the lives of those dear to her. How gladly would she have made her own these lines of Caussade:

> *The history of that divine drama which consists in the life led by Jesus in holy souls . . . can only be guessed at by our faith. . . . The holy souls are the paper, their sufferings and actions are the ink. The Holy Spirit, with the pen of his activity, writes in*

them a living gospel.

And the following paragraphs—among Caussade's finest—might well be taken as a complete summary of her life:

Their life, though extraordinary in its perfection, shows nothing on the outside but what is common and very ordinary: they fulfil the duties of religion and of their state; others, as far as appearances go, do the same as they. Examine the rest of their lives: you will find nothing striking or special; they are made up of the ordinary course of events. What distinguishes them—the dependence in which they live on the will of God which arranges everything for them—does not fall under observation. . . . When God gives himself to the soul in this way, the ordinary sequence of life becomes extraordinary. This is why nothing extraordinary appears outwardly; because it is extraordinary in itself and consequently does not need the ornament of marvels which have nothing to do with it.

A final point may be noted. It has often been remarked that the great contemplatives, whatever theological formation they may have received, all use the same language when speaking of the action of grace on the soul. Caussade is no exception, and though he never develops a theory, his scheme of thought is consistent. I will give some of the most typical passages without comment, to direct the attention of those who may be interested in the subject. His leading thesis is as follows:

God and the soul perform together a work the success of which depends on the divine Workman, and can be compromised only by the soul's infidelity.

He explains this at greater length elsewhere:

The soul (of the contemplative), *like a musical instrument, receives nothing and produces nothing except in so far as the intimate operation of God occupies it in a state of passivity or applies it to some external action. Such external application is accompanied by a co-operation which from the soul's side is free and active but from God's side is infused and mystical.*

And so, as the soul grows in grace and self-abandonment,

It forms insensibly a habit of acting always by the instinct (so to speak) of God,

and thus:

The unique and infallible movement of the divine action always applies the soul in its simplicity exactly, and it corresponds always very perfectly to this intimate direction. . . . Sometimes it does this with advertence and sometimes without, being moved by obscure instincts to speak, act and abstain without other reasons,

and so:

We must learn to let ourselves go passively under the divine action, allowing the Holy Spirit to act in our interior, without knowing what he is doing, and even being content not to know.

It need scarcely be repeated that Caussade is speaking here the wisdom of God among the perfect; by them he will be understood; the rest of us may reverence his words even where we do not fully appreciate their meaning.

And so, I think, we may approach Père de Caussade —'the incomparable Caussade', as Bremond calls him —looking back to St John of the Cross and St Francis de Sales and forward to St Teresa of the Infant Jesus. If I have, in these pages of introduction, extracted and emphasized almost solely those sentences in which he outlines his theories, it is because a teacher must ultimately be judged by the great principles of his doctrine. But it is not the least merit of Caussade that he may be read by those to whom theory means little, and who ask of a book nothing but that it may lead them to God.

1933

A BIOGRAPHICAL NOTE

JEAN PIERRE DE CAUSSADE was born in 1675 and entered the Jesuit novitiate in Toulouse at the age of eighteen. After spending a year or so in the novitiate he was sent to teach classics in the Jesuit college in Aurillac. In 1702 he began his theological studies, was ordained priest in 1705, completed his theological studies the following year and took his final vows in 1708. From 1708 to 1714 he taught grammar, physics and logic in the Jesuit college in Toulouse, and then ceased teaching in order to devote himself to the itinerant career of a missioner and preacher.

Between the years 1715 and 1729 he was stationed successively in the residences of Rodez, Montauban, Auch, Clermont, Annecy, Puy and Beauvais. For the next two years he was in Lorraine, and it was during this period that he made his first contact with the nuns of the Order of the Visitation in Nancy, to whom we are indebted for having preserved his letters and the notes of his conferences. In 1731 he was sent as spiritual director to the seminary in Albi, but two years later was back in Nancy in charge of the Jesuit Retreat house there. During his seven years in this office he gave frequent conferences to the Visitation nuns and undertook the personal direction of several of them. The Superior of the convent at this time was Mother de Rosen to whom many of his letters were written. She was a woman of great intelligence and culture, and of high mystical attainments, like her trusted junior, Sister de Vioménil.

In 1740 Fr de Caussade was back in Toulouse. Then from 1741 to 1743 he was Rector of the Jesuit college in Perpignan, and for the following three years he occupied a similar post in the college in Albi. His letters during these years show him struggling with wry humour to resign himself to the office of superior which he seems to have heartily disliked. In 1746 he returned to the House of Professed in Toulouse and acted as spiritual director in the seminary there. His blindness, which appears to have been threatening him for some years, grew worse, but he bore it with courageous fortitude and in the spirit of his own great principle of self-abandonment to the will of God. He died in 1751 at the age of seventy-six.

Apart from his letters and conference notes which were preserved by the nuns of the Visitation, Caussade's contemporaries appear to have left no note of him beyond the bare statement of his whereabouts as given above. His career seems to have been typical of most other men of his Order, and again typically his name occurs once only in the Jesuit menology in a passing allusion in a biographical account of his better-known colleague, P. Antoine. Yet in spite of this lack of contemporary evidence we can gain a good impression of the man from his works.

The only book he published in his own lifetime was the 'Spiritual Instructions on the various states of prayer according to the teaching of Bossuet' (published in English under the title of *On Prayer* by Burns Oates and Washbourne). This book appeared anonymously in 1741 at Perpignan and was for a time attributed to his popular contemporary, P. Antoine, S.J. The style is dry and in the form of a catechism, but it betrays profound spiritual discernment and his own abiding preoccupation with the deeper problems of the spiritual life. Possibly also it was written to combat any suspicion of his being a Quietist, for the spiritual world of France was still shaking from the great controversy between the two Archbishops, Bossuet and Fénelon, in which the latter had been overwhelmed, and had later been condemned by Rome for Semi-Quietism.

But Caussade reveals himself more clearly in the treatise on Self-abandonment and in his letters. The history of these works is somewhat peculiar. They were not published by Caussade himself or even during his lifetime. The treatise was put together from notes of his conferences which the nuns of the Visitation convent in Nancy took down and circulated among their other convents. After some years these notes were published in various mutilated forms until Fr Ramière, S.J., took the work in hand, putting them into logical order and publishing them together with the letters in 1861. Since that time they have gone through no less than twenty-five editions, with slight emendations and additions.

In the treatise we get a good picture of Caussade. His clarity, fluency and ease of style show us a man who is master of his subject. He is also passionately in earnest about it and passionately eager to communicate it to others. There is nothing cold or formal about him; indeed at moments his burning zeal and conviction lift his style to a moving and urgent eloquence.

In his letters he shows himself to be not only a teacher but also a man who fervently practises the art of prayer for himself, and has suffered and passed through the tremendous experiences of the spiritual life in his own soul. His direction of souls in these lofty and difficult ways is authoritative and firm with the authority that comes from profound study and intimate personal experience. But beneath his intensity and his almost relentless drive there is always the calm serenity and poise of a well-balanced character, and the human kindliness of a sensitive director of souls.

The style is the man, and from the style of the letters

we get a picture of a man of delightful spontaneity, of verve and vigour, but tender, sympathetic and humorous. He is subtle but logical, humble but sure, straight, forceful and firm yet gently persuasive and always encouraging and patient. Obviously Caussade was a man of fine natural character and charm, and of high spiritual attainments and mystical gifts. No wonder his treatise and letters have become one of the favourites among spiritual classics.

Perhaps a warning should be given to readers of the letters. We must remember that these were written for the most part to nuns who were already far advanced in the spiritual life, and so they take for granted the essential but elementary fundamentals of religious life. These of course are of first importance and must not be neglected or underestimated by even the most advanced, and much less so by beginners like ourselves. But, read with this caution in mind, the letters can be enjoyed and used by everyone.

John Joyce, s.j.

THE VIRTUE OF SELF-ABANDONMENT

CHAPTER ONE

SANCTITY CONSISTS IN FIDELITY TO THE ORDER ESTABLISHED BY GOD AND IN SELF-ABANDONMENT TO HIS ACTION

§1. *The sanctity of the saints of the Old Law, as likewise that of St Joseph and our Lady, consisted wholly in fidelity to the order established by God*

God still speaks to us today as he spoke to our fathers, when there were no spiritual directors or set methods. Then, spirituality consisted in fidelity to the designs of God, for it had not yet been reduced to an art and explained in a lofty and detailed manner with many rules, maxims and instructions. Doubtless our present needs demand this, but it was not so in former ages when men were more upright and simple. Then it was enough for those who led a spiritual life to see that each moment brought with it a duty to be faithfully fulfilled. On that duty the whole of their attention was fixed at each successive moment, like the hand of a clock which marks each moment of the hour. Under God's unceasing guidance their spirit turned without conscious effort to each new duty as it was presented to them by God each hour of the day.

Such were the hidden springs of Mary's conduct, for she was of all creatures the most utterly submissive to God. Her reply to the angel when she said simply: *Fiat mihi secundum verbum tuum,* contained all the mystical theology of our ancestors. Everything was reduced, as indeed it is today, to the complete and utter self-abandonment of the soul to God's will under whatever form it was manifested.

This beautiful and lofty disposition of Mary's soul is admirably revealed in those simple words: *Fiat mihi.* Note how perfectly they agree with those words which our Lord wishes us to have always on our lips and in our hearts: *Fiat voluntas tua.* It is true that what was asked of Mary at that moment was something very glorious for her. But all the splendour of that glory would have had no effect on her had she not seen in it the will of God which alone was able to move her.

It was this divine will which ruled her every act. Whatever her occupations, commonplace or lofty, they were in her eyes but external signs, sometimes clear, sometimes obscure, under which she saw the means both of glorifying God and of acknowledging the action of the Almighty. Her spirit, transported with joy, looked on everything she had to do or to suffer at each moment as a gift from him who fills with good things the hearts which hunger for him alone and not for created things.

§2. *The duties of each moment are shadows beneath which the divine action lies concealed*

'The power of the Most High shall overshadow thee,' said the angel to Mary. This shadow beneath which the power of God conceals itself in order to bring Jesus Christ to souls, is the duty, attraction or cross which every moment brings. These are in fact but shadows similar to those in nature which spread themselves like a veil over visible objects and hide them from us. Thus in the moral and supernatural order the duties of each moment conceal under their outward appearances the true reality of the divine will which alone is worthy of our attention. It was in this light that Mary regarded them. As these shadows spread over her faculties, far from causing her any illusion, they filled her with faith in him who is unchanging. Draw back, archangel, you are only a shadow; your moment passes and you disappear. Mary moves beyond you; Mary goes forward unceasingly. From now on you are left far behind her. But the Holy Spirit, who under the visible form of this mission has entered into her, will never leave her.

There are few extraordinary features in the external life of the Blessed Virgin. At least Holy Scripture does not record any. Her life is represented as externally very simple and ordinary. She does and experiences the same things as other people in her state of life. She goes to visit her cousin Elizabeth, as her other relations do. She takes shelter in a stable: a natural consequence of her poverty. She returns to Nazareth after having fled from the persecution of Herod; Jesus and Joseph live there with her, supporting themselves by the work of their hands. This provides their daily bread, but what is the divine food with which this material bread feeds the faith of Mary and Joseph? What is the sacrament of each of their sacred moments? What treasures of grace are contained in each of these moments underneath the commonplace appearance of the events that fill them? Outwardly these events are no different from those which happen to everyone, but the interior invisible element discerned by faith is nothing less than God himself performing great works. O bread of angels, heavenly manna, the pearl of the Gospels, the sacrament of the present moment! You present God in such lowly forms as the manger, the hay and straw! But to whom do you give him? *Esurientes reples bonis*. 'You fill the hungry with good things.' God reveals himself to the humble in the humblest things, while the great who never penetrate beneath the surface do not discover him even in great events.

§3. *How much easier holiness would become if it were regarded from this point of view*

If the work of our sanctification presents us with difficulties apparently so insurmountable, it is because we do not look at it in the right way. In reality holiness consists in one thing alone, namely, fidelity to God's plan. And this fidelity is equally within everyone's capacity in both its active and passive practice.

The active practice of fidelity consists in accomplishing the duties imposed on us by the general laws of God and the Church, and by the particular state of life which we have embraced. Passive fidelity consists in the loving acceptance of all that God sends us at every moment.

Which of these two requirements of holiness is beyond our strength? Not active fidelity, since the duties imposed by it cease to be such when they are really beyond our powers. If the state of your health does not allow you to hear Mass, you are under no obligation to do so. It is the same with all positive precepts, namely, those which prescribe duties to be done. The only precepts to which no exceptions can be permitted are those which forbid the doing of things that are evil in themselves, for it is never permissible to do evil.

Can anything be easier or more reasonable? What excuse can we plead? Yet this is all that God demands of the soul in the work of its sanctification. He demands it from the high and the low, from the strong and the weak; in a word, from all, always and everywhere. It is true then that he asks from us only what is simple and easy, for it is sufficient to possess this simple fund of goodwill in order to attain to eminent holiness.

If over and above the commandments he puts before us the counsels as a more perfect goal of our endeavour, he is always careful to accommodate the practice of the counsels to our position and character. The attractions of grace which facilitate the practice of the counsels are the chief sign that he is calling us to follow them. He never presses anyone beyond his strength or aptitudes. Once more, what could be more just?

All you who aim at perfection and are tempted to discouragement by what you read in the lives of the saints and by what is prescribed in certain books of piety; you who are appalled by the terrible ideas which you form of perfection, it is for your consolation that God wills me to write this. Learn now what you seemingly do not know.

This God of goodness has put within easy reach all the things which are necessary and common in the natural order, such as earth, air and water. Nothing is more necessary than breathing, sleeping and eating; and nothing is easier. Love and fidelity are no less necessary in the supernatural order; therefore they cannot be so difficult to acquire as is imagined. Look at your life. What is it made up of? Of innumerable unimportant actions. It is just with these very things, so trifling in themselves, that God is pleased to be satisfied. They are the share that falls to the soul in the work of its perfection. God himself makes his meaning too clear for us to doubt this. 'Fear God and keep his commandments, for this is the whole duty of man.' Here is all that a man has to do on his side, here is what active fidelity consists in. If man fulfils his part, God will do the rest. Grace will take full control of him, and the wonders that it will work in him surpass all man's understanding. For the ear has not heard, nor the eye seen, nor the heart felt what God plans in his mind, resolves upon in his will, and executes by his power in souls that abandon themselves to him.

The passive part of holiness is even more easy, for it consists merely in accepting what most frequently cannot be avoided, and in suffering with love, that is to say with resignation and sweetness, what is too often endured with weariness and discontent.

Here then once more is the whole of sanctity. Here is the grain of mustard seed of which the fruits are lost because we cannot recognize it on account of its smallness. Here is the drachma of the Gospel parable, the treasure which we never find because we imagine it to be too far away to be sought.

Do not ask me what is the secret of finding this treasure. There is no secret. This treasure is everywhere. It is offered to us at every moment and in every place. All creatures, both friendly and hostile, pour it out with prodigality and make it pervade every faculty of our body and soul, right to the depths of our heart. We have only to open our mouths and they will be filled. Divine activity floods the whole universe; it pervades all creatures; it flows over them. Wherever they are, it is there; it precedes, accompanies and follows them. We have but to allow ourselves to be carried forward on the crest of its waves.

Would to God that kings and their ministers, princes of the Church and of the world, priests, soldiers, tradesmen and labourers, in a word all men, understood how easy it is for them to attain great holiness! They have only to fulfil the simple duties of the Catholic faith and of their state of life, to accept with submission the crosses that go with those duties, and to submit with faith and love to the designs of Providence in everything that is constantly being presented to them to do and to endure, without searching for anything themselves. This is the spirituality that sanctified the patriarchs and prophets before so many different methods and masters of the spiritual life were introduced. This is the spirituality of all ages and states of life which assuredly cannot be made holy in a nobler, more wonderful and easier manner than by simply making use of what God, the sovereign director of souls, gives them to do or suffer at each moment.[1]

§4. *Perfection does not consist in understanding God's designs but in submitting to them*

God's designs, God's good pleasure, the will of God, the action of God and his grace are all one and the same thing in this life. They are God working in the soul to make it like himself. Perfection is nothing else than the faithful co-operation of the soul with the work of God, and it begins, grows and is consummated in our souls secretly and without our being aware of it.

Theology is full of ideas and expressions explaining the marvels of this ultimate state in each soul in accordance with its captivity. A man may know all the theory of it, may speak and write admirably on the subject, and instruct and direct souls, but if his knowledge remains merely theoretical, then compared with those who attain the goal of God's design without knowing the theory of it in whole or in part, or without being able to discourse on it, he is like a sick doctor in comparison with simple people who are in perfect health.

When God's designs and will are embraced with simplicity by a faithful soul, they produce this divine

[1] It would be a misunderstanding of the author's thought to suppose that he wishes to urge anyone to embark on the spiritual life without a director. He himself elsewhere says expressly that in order to be capable of doing without a director, one must already have had long and skilful direction. Still less does he seek to turn anyone away from the practices in use in the Church for ridding oneself of vices and acquiring virtues. What he means, and what cannot be too frequently said, is that the direction given by divine Providence is the first and best of all, and that the most necessary and sanctifying of all spiritual practices is the faithful carrying out and the loving acceptance of everything that this fatherly Providence ordains us to do and to suffer.

state in it without its knowing it; just as medicine taken obediently by a sick man effects his cure even though he neither knows nor is capable of knowing anything about medicine. Similarly, as it is fire and not the philosophy or scientific knowledge of fire that warms us, so it is the will and designs of God that produce sanctity in our souls and not intellectual speculation about this principle and its effects. If we wish to quench our thirst, we must lay aside books which explain thirst, and take a drink. By itself, curiosity for knowledge can only make one thirstier. Thus, when we thirst for holiness, curiosity for theoretical knowledge of it can only drive it further from us. We must put speculation on one side, and with simplicity drink everything that God's designs present to us in actions and sufferings. What happens to us each moment by God's design is for us the holiest, best and most divine thing.

§5. *Spiritual reading and other exercises of piety sanctify us only in so far as they are the channels of God's action*

The whole essence of the spiritual life consists in recognizing the designs of God for us at the present moment. All reading that is chosen by us apart from God's designs is harmful to us; the designs and will of God are the grace which works in the depths of our hearts through the books we read as through everything else we do. Apart from God, books are merely useless externals, and being devoid for us of the life-giving power of God's plan, they succeed only in emptying the heart by the very satisfaction which they give to the mind.

This divine will, working in the soul of a simple ignorant girl by means of a few ordinary sufferings and actions, produces in the depths of her heart this mysterious fulfilment of supernatural life without putting into her mind ideas which might make her conceited. While on the contrary, a proud man who reads spiritual books only from curiosity and without any regard for the will of God receives only the dead letter into his mind, and his heart grows ever drier and harder.

The will and designs of God are the life of the soul no matter what the appearance under which the soul receives them or applies them to itself.

In whatever manner this divine will touches the mind, it nourishes the soul and continually enlarges it by giving it what is best for it at every moment. These happy effects are produced not by any particular event as such, but by God's design for each individual moment. What was best for the moment which has just passed, is so no longer because it is no longer the will of God; this now presents itself under other appearances and forms the duty of the present moment. It is this duty which, in whatever guise it may appear, is the most sanctifying for the soul.

If the duty of the present moment is to read, then reading will produce this mysterious fulfilment in the depths of the soul. If the divine will bids us turn from reading to the duty of contemplation, this duty develops the 'new man' in the depths of the heart, whereas to continue reading would be harmful and useless. If the divine will withdraws us from contemplation in order to hear confessions etc., even for a long time, this duty is the means of forming Jesus Christ in the depths of the heart, and all the sweetness of contemplation would only serve to drive him out.

It is the designs of God that are the fulfilment of all our moments. They manifest themselves in a thousand different ways which thus become our successive duties, and form, increase and perfect the 'new man' in us until we attain the full stature destined for us by divine wisdom. This mysterious growth in age of Jesus Christ in our hearts is the end and fulfilment produced by the designs of God; it is the fruit of his grace and his divine goodness.

This fruit, as we have said, is produced, fed and increased by the duties which are successively presented to us and are filled with the will of God. In performing these duties we are always sure of possessing the 'better part', for this holy will is itself the 'better part'. We have only to allow it freedom to work in us and abandon ourselves blindly to it in perfect confidence. It is infinitely wise, infinitely powerful, infinitely beneficent towards souls who place their hope in it utterly without reserve, who love and seek nothing but it alone, and who believe with unshakeable faith and confidence that what it does at each moment is the best, without looking elsewhere for something more or something less, and without pausing to consider the connection between God's designs and external things, for this is the mere seeking of self-love.

The will of God is the essential and real element and the power in all things; it is the will of God that adjusts and adapts them to the soul. Without it, all is nothingness, emptiness, lies and vanity, the mere letter without the spirit, empty husks and death. The will of God is the salvation, health and life of body and soul no matter what the external appearance of the thing to which it is applied. We must not therefore examine the suitability of things to mind and body in order to assess their value, for this is of little importance; it is the will of God which gives to things, whatever they may be, the power to form Jesus Christ in the depths of our hearts. We must not dictate to God's will nor set limits to its action, for it is all-powerful.

Whatever ideas the mind may choose to be filled with, whatever the feelings of the body; even if the mind be afflicted with distractions and worries, and the body with sickness and death, nevertheless the divine will is always for the present moment the life of the body and the soul, for in whatever state they are, both are ultimately sustained only by the divine will. Without it bread is poison; with it poison is a salutary remedy. Without it books do nothing but darken the mind, and with it darkness becomes light. It is everything that is good and true in all things. And in all things it gives us God, and God is the infinite being who takes the place of all things for the soul that possesses him.

§6. *The mind and other human means are useful only in so far as they serve as instruments of the divine action*

The mind, together with everything that depends on it, is bent upon holding first place among the means of divine action, and it has to be reduced to the last place like a dangerous slave. A man wholly devoted to God can draw from it great advantages if he knows how to use it; but it can also do great harm if it is not kept under control. When the soul longs for the use of creatures, grace makes it understand that divine action is sufficient for it; when the soul wishes to abandon created means at the wrong time, divine action shows it that these things are instruments which must not be taken up or abandoned on its own judgment, but must be accepted and adapted with simplicity to God's designs, making use of all things with detachment as one not using them, and as being deprived of everything yet lacking nothing.

Divine action, being limitless in its plenitude, can take possession of a soul only to the extent to which that soul is emptied of all trust in its own action, for such self-confidence is a spurious fullness that excludes divine action.

This is the obstacle most likely to impede divine

action, namely that which is found in the soul itself, for in the case of external obstacles the divine action can, when it chooses, convert them into useful means. Everything is equally useful and useless to it. Without it everything is as nothing, and with it nothing becomes everything. Meditation, contemplation, vocal prayers, interior silence, acts of the faculties of the soul, whether accompanied by emotional feelings, and whether distinctly or less clearly perceived, a life of retirement or an active one, all these things may be valuable in themselves, but the best of all for the soul is what God wills at this particular moment, and all else must be regarded by the soul with perfect indifference as being nothing at all.

Thus, seeing only God in all things, the soul must take or leave them all at his will so as to live, to grow and to hope only in his designs, and not in things which have no power or value except through him. It must say like St Paul always and of everything: 'Lord, what wilt thou have me do?' Not this thing or that, but: 'All that thou wishest!' The mind likes one thing, the body another, but, Lord, I desire nothing but your holy will. Prayer or action, vocal or mental prayer, whether active or passive, in the darkness of faith or in the light of understanding, with a special gift of grace or by ordinary grace, all these things are as nothing, Lord, for it is your will that gives them all their real and sole value. Your will alone is the object of my devotion, and not created things, however elevated and sublime they may be; for the fulfilment of grace is the perfection of the heart and not of the mind.

The presence of God which sanctifies our souls is the indwelling of the Blessed Trinity, who take up their abode in the depths of our hearts when we submit to the divine will; for the presence of God that results from contemplation effects this intimate union in us only in the same way as other things which are part of God's design. Contemplation however ranks first among these things because it is the greatest means of uniting ourselves to God when the divine will bids us make use of it.

We are perfectly right therefore to esteem and love contemplation and other practices of piety, provided that our esteem and attraction to them are directed wholly to God who in his infinite goodness wills to use these means in order to give himself to our souls. In entertaining a prince's suite, one entertains the prince himself. It would be an insult to him to show no regard for his officers on the plea of wanting him alone.

§7. *Genuine and stable peace is to be found only in submission to divine action*

The soul that is not attached to the will of God alone, will find neither contentment nor sanctification in the various means which it may try nor in even the most excellent practices of piety. If what God himself selects for you does not satisfy you, what other hand than his can serve you as you desire? If you are disgusted with the food prepared for you by the divine will itself, what other food will not seem insipid to so depraved a taste? A soul can be truly nourished, strengthened, purified, enriched and sanctified only by the divine plenitude of the present moment. What more do you want? Since all that is good is here, why seek it elsewhere? Do you know better than God? He ordains it thus, why therefore desire it otherwise? Can his wisdom and goodness be mistaken? Ought you not to be convinced of the excellence of whatever accords with this divine wisdom and goodness? Do you think you will find peace by struggling against the Almighty? Is it not rather this very resistance which we too often make almost without admitting the fact to ourselves, that is the cause of all our agitation?

It is indeed right that the soul that is not satisfied with the fullness of divine action in the present moment, should be punished by being unable to find contentment in anything else. If books, the example of the saints and spiritual discourses disturb our peace of soul, or if they fill the soul without satisfying it, this is a sign that we have strayed from the path of pure self-abandonment to divine action and that we are filling ourselves with these things in a spirit of self-seeking; there is then no room for God. We must get rid of these things for they are an obstacle to grace. But when divine action prescribes these things, the soul accepts them like everything else, that is to say, as God's plan for us. The soul takes them just as they are, accepting merely the use of them in order to remain faithful to God's design; and as soon as their moment is past it abandons them and turns contentedly to the duties of the next moment. Nothing in truth is really good for me but the action which agrees with God's design. I cannot find elsewhere any means, however good in itself, that is better adapted for my sanctification or capable of giving me peace.

§8. *The perfection of souls and the excellence of various states of life are measured by their fidelity to God's designs*

God's design imparts a supernatural and divine value to everything for the soul that conforms to that design. All it imposes, all it contains, and every object to which it extends becomes holy and perfect, for its power has no limits; everything it touches, it makes divine.

But in order not to stray either to right or left, the soul must not follow any inspiration, which it believes it has received from God, before making certain that this inspiration is not diverting it from the duties of its state. These duties are the surest manifestation of God's design, and nothing must be preferred to them. In them there is nothing to be feared, nothing to be excluded or preferred. The moments employed in fulfilling these duties are most precious and salutary for the soul by the very fact that they give it the undoubted assurance that it is accomplishing the good pleasure of its God.

The whole virtue of what is called holiness lies in these designs of God; nothing therefore must be rejected, nothing sought after, but everything must be accepted from his hand and nothing without him. Books, the counsels of the wise, vocal prayers and interior affections, all these things instruct us, direct us and unite us with him provided that God's will prescribes them. Quietism is in error when it despises these means and all use of the senses, for there are souls whom God wishes to go by this road always; and this is shown clearly enough by their state of life and spiritual leanings. It is useless to imagine methods of self-abandonment from which all personal activity is excluded; when the divine plan prescribes action, holiness for us lies in activity.

Beyond the duties imposed on each one by his state of life, God may require certain actions which are not included among these duties, although in no way contrary to them. In such cases spiritual attraction and inspiration are the indication of the designs of God, and the most perfect course for souls whom God is leading in this way is to add what is inspired to what is commanded, observing however the precautions which inspiration requires, so as not to interfere with the duties of one's state or with what belongs purely to Providence.

God makes saints as he pleases, but they are all made according to his plan, and all must be submissive to this plan. This submission is true self-abandonment, and it is the most perfect of all ways.

The duties imposed by their state of life and by God's Providence are common to all the saints and are God's mark on them all in general. They live hidden in obscurity, for the world is so deadly that they steer clear of its dangers; but this does not constitute their sanctity; it consists entirely in their submission to God's designs. The more absolute this submission becomes, the greater is their sanctity. We must not think that those in whom God causes virtues to be displayed in unusual and extraordinary ways and by unquestionable spiritual attractions and inspirations follow the path of self-abandonment any the less on that account. Once God's design imposes these extraordinary acts on them as a duty, they must not be content merely with the duties of their state and of ordinary Providence, for then they would not be abandoning themselves to God and his will; his will would no longer rule all their moments, and their moments would not be the will of God. They must reach out and extend themselves to the further measure of God's designs along this way which is traced out for them by spiritual attraction. The inspiration of grace must become for them a duty, and they must be faithful to it. As there are souls whose whole duty is defined for them by external laws and who must confine themselves to these because it is God's design to restrict them within these bounds, so there are others who beside their external duties should also be faithful to the interior law which the Holy Spirit imprints on their hearts.

But which are the holiest? It is mere vain curiosity to try to find out. Each must follow the way that is marked out for him. Perfection consists in complete submission to God's designs and in carrying out unfailingly what is most perfect in them.

Sanctity consists in fidelity and self-abandonment

To compare the different states in themselves takes us no further, for it is not in the quantity or quality of what is commanded that holiness is to be sought. If self-love is the motive on which we act, or if it is not corrected when we become aware of it, we shall always be poor in the midst of an abundance that is not of God's design. However, to give some answer to the question, it is my opinion that holiness corresponds to the love we have for God's good pleasure; the more his will and designs are loved, no matter what the means they ordain, the greater is the sanctity. This is seen in Jesus, Mary and Joseph; for in their personal lives there was more love than grandeur, more form than matter; and we are not told that these holy persons sought out holy things and circumstances, but only holiness in all their circumstances.

It must therefore be concluded that there is no particular path which is the most perfect one; the most perfect in general is submission to God's designs whether in the performance of external duties or in interior dispositions.

§9. *Conclusion of the first chapter. How easy holiness becomes when this doctrine is well understood*

I believe that if souls aiming seriously at holiness were taught to follow this way, they would be spared a great deal of trouble. I say this for people in the world as well as for souls specially privileged by Providence. If the former knew the merit hidden in what each moment of the day brings them, I mean their daily duties and the actions proper to their state of life; if the latter could only persuade themselves that the essence of sanctity consists in things which seem of no importance to them and which they even consider alien to it; if both these classes of souls understood that in order to rise to the highest degree of perfection the crosses, which by divine Providence are furnished them at every instant by their state of life, open to them a far surer and shorter road than extraordinary states and actions, and that the true philosopher's stone is submission to the designs of God which transmutes into divine gold all their occupations, their worries and sufferings, how happy they would be! What consolation and courage they would draw from the thought that in order to gain God's friendship and all the glories of heaven, they need neither do nor suffer anything more than what they are already doing and suffering and that what they waste and reckon worthless would be enough to purchase eminent holiness!

O my God, how I should wish to be the missionary of your holy will and teach everyone that there is nothing so easy, so ordinary and so ready to everyone's hand as holiness! How I should like to be able to make them understand that just as the good thief and the bad thief had no different things to do and suffer in order to be saints, so two people, one of whom is worldly and the other leading an interior and spiritual life, have, neither of them, more to do or suffer than the other. The one who sanctifies himself acquires eternal happiness in doing with submission to your holy will the same things that the other who damns himself does through self-will; and the latter damns himself in suffering unwillingly and rebelliously the very same things that the other who saves his soul endures with resignation. The heart alone makes the difference.

O beloved souls who read this, the cost will be no greater for you. Do what you are doing now, suffer what you are suffering now; to do all this with holiness, nothing need be changed but your hearts. By the heart is meant the will, and sanctity therefore consists in willing what happens to us by God's design. Yes, holiness of heart is a simple *fiat*, a simple conformity of the will to God's will. What can be easier? For who can fail to love a will so lovable and good? Let us love it then, and through this love alone everything in us will be made divine.

CHAPTER TWO

THE DIVINE ACTION WORKS UNCEASINGLY AT THE SANCTIFICATION OF SOULS

§1. *The divine action is present everywhere and always, although it is only visible to the eye of faith*

All creatures are living in the hand of God; the senses perceive only the action of the creature, but faith sees the action of God in everything—faith believes that Jesus Christ is alive in everything and operates throughout the whole course of the centuries; faith believes that the briefest moment and the tiniest atom contain a portion of Christ's hidden life and his mysterious action. The action of creatures is a veil concealing the profound mysteries of the divine action. Jesus Christ after his resurrection took his disciples by surprise in his apparitions, he presented himself to them under appearances which disguised him; and as soon as he had revealed himself, he disappeared. This very same Jesus, always living and active, still takes by surprise souls whose faith is not sufficiently pure and penetrating.

There is no moment at which God does not present himself under the guise of some suffering, some consolation or some duty. All that occurs within us, around us and by our means covers and hides his divine action. His action is there, most really and certainly present, but in an invisible manner, the result of which is that we are always being taken by surprise and that we only recognize his operation after it has passed. Could we pierce the veil and were we vigilant and attentive, God would reveal himself continuously to us and we should rejoice in his action in everything that happens to us.

At every occurrence we should say: *Dominus est.* It is the Lord; and in all circumstances we should find a gift from God: we should consider creatures as very feeble instruments in the hands of an almighty worker, and we should recognize without difficulty that nothing is lacking to us and that God's constant care leads him to give us each instant what is suited to us. If we had faith, we should welcome all creatures; we should, as it were, caress them and thank them interiorly for contributing so favourably to our perfection when applied by the hand of God.

If we lived uninterruptedly by the life of faith, we should be in continual contact with God, we should speak with him face to face. As the air is the medium for transmitting our thoughts and words to others, so all our deeds or sufferings would transmit to us the thoughts and words of God; they would be but the embodiment of his words giving them their external expression; for us, all would be holy and excellent. This union with God will be established in heaven by glory; faith will establish it on earth and the only difference is in our mode of reception.

Faith is the interpreter of God; without the illumination which it brings, nothing can be understood of the language in which creatures speak to us. That language is a cypher in which nothing is apparent but confusion; it is a thorn-bush from which no one could imagine God speaking. But faith makes us see, as in the case of Moses, the fire of divine charity burning in the midst of the thorns; faith gives us the key to the cypher and enables us to discover in that confusion the marvels of heavenly wisdom. Faith gives a face as of heaven to the whole earth, and by it our hearts are ravished and transported to converse in heaven.

Faith is the light of time: alone it attains truth without seeing it; it touches what it does not feel, it beholds this world as if it were not there, seeing something quite different to what appears on the surface. Faith is the key of the treasury, the key of the abyss of divine wisdom, the key of the science of God. It is faith that gives the lie to all creation, it is by faith that God reveals and manifests himself in all things. It is faith that divinizes things, which lifts the veil and reveals to us eternal truth.

All that we see is lies and vanity; the truth of things is in God. What a difference between the ideas of God and our illusions! How can it be that though we are continually warned that every passing event in the world is but a shadow, a figure, a mystery of faith, we always behave in a merely human way and judge events by our natural understanding of them with the result that they remain an enigma? We fall into the snare like fools instead of lifting our eyes and ascending to the principle, the source, the origin of things, where everything has another name and other qualities, where everything is supernatural, divine and sanctifying; where everything is part of the plenitude of Jesus Christ; where each occurrence is a stone of the heavenly Jerusalem, where everything is a means of entrance into that marvellous city. We live as we see and as we feel; and we render useless that light of faith which would lead us so surely through the labyrinth of clouds and images among which we lose our way like idiots, because we do not walk by the light of faith which desires nothing but God and what is his and which lives for ever by him, passing beyond and abandoning what is but an image.

§2. *The more repugnant the appearances under which it is concealed, the more clearly is the divine action visible to the eye of faith*

The soul illuminated by faith is very far from judging things as do those who measure them by their senses, being ignorant of the inestimable treasure they conceal. He who knows that a certain person in disguise is the King welcomes him in a very different manner from one who seeing the exterior aspect of an ordinary man treats him according to his appearance. Similarly, the soul that sees the will of God in the smallest things or in the most distressing and fatal events, accepts them all with equal joy, gladness and respect. What other people fear and fly from in horror is received by this soul with honour. It throws its gates wide open in welcome. Though the guest's equipage may be small and the senses despise it, yet the heart none the less reveres the royal majesty beneath the mean trappings; and the more his royal majesty abases himself to come in this hidden and humble way, the more deeply is the heart penetrated with love.

I cannot express the feelings of the heart when it welcomes the divine will, so diminished in glory, so poor, so annihilated. How the beautiful heart of Mary was penetrated by this poverty of a God, this annihilation to the point of dwelling in a stable, sleeping on a little straw, to the point of weeping and trembling! Ask the inhabitants of Bethlehem, see what they think of this child: if he were lodged in a palace surrounded with the state of a prince, they would pay their court to him. But ask the same question of Mary, Joseph, the Magi, the shepherds: they will tell you that they find in this extreme poverty something which makes God greater and more lovable. The very deficiency of material things enhances, increases and enriches faith: the less for the eyes, the more for the soul. To adore Jesus on Thabor, to love the will of God in extraordinary things, does not indicate as excellent a life of faith as to love the will of God in ordinary circumstances and to love Jesus on the Cross, for faith is only living at its best when sensible appearances contradict and attempt to destroy it. This war of the senses renders faith more gloriously triumphant. To find God as good in the tiniest and most ordinary events as in the greatest is to have not an ordinary but a great and extraordinary faith. To be content with the present moment is to appreciate and adore the divine will in all we have to do and suffer in the events which reveal it to us. Souls in these dispositions adore God with redoubled love and respect in the most humiliating circumstances; nothing hides him from the piercing eye of their faith. The more the senses declare: there can be no God there, the more these souls hug to their breast the myrrh of their suffering; nothing astonishes them, nothing disgusts them.

Mary will witness the flight of the Apostles; but she will remain herself constant at the foot of the Cross. She will recognize her Son, no matter how disfigured he may be by spittle and wounds, for, contrariwise, his disfiguring wounds make him the more adorable and lovable to his tender mother; the more he is blasphemed, the greater will be her veneration. The life of faith is nothing else than a continual pursuit of God through everything that disguises, misrepresents and, so to speak, destroys and annihilates him. It is, indeed, the reproduction of the life of Mary who from the stable to Calvary remains attached to a God whom everyone fails to recognize, abandons and persecutes. In the same way men of faith pass through and beyond a continual succession of veils, shadows, appearances and, as it were, deaths, all of which do their best to make the will of God unrecognizable, but they pursue and love the divine will unto the death of the Cross. They know that shadows must always be abandoned in order to follow this divine Sun who from his rising unto his going down, however dark or heavy may be the clouds that hide him, enlightens, warms and makes to glow with love the faithful hearts who bless, praise and contemplate him at all points of his mysterious orbit.

Hasten then always, faithful souls, happy and tireless after your beloved Spouse who walks with giant's steps from one end of the heavens to the other; nothing is hidden from his sight. He walks over the tiniest blades of grass as well as over cedars. He passes over grains of sand as well as over mountains. Wherever you can step, he has passed, and in order to find him wherever you may be, you have but to pursue him incessantly.

How delightful the peace one enjoys when one has learned by faith to see God in this way through all creatures as through a transparent veil! Darkness becomes light and bitterness sweet. Faith by showing us the truth of things changes their ugliness into beauty and their malice into goodness: faith is the mother of gentleness, confidence and joy; she can have only tenderness and compassion towards her enemies who enrich her so greatly at their own cost. The more cruel the action of the creature, the more profitable does the action of God make it for the soul who endures it. While the human tool does its best to injure, the divine artificer, in whose hands it does its work, makes use of that very malice to remove from the soul what is injurious. The will of God has nothing but sweetness, favours and treasures for souls submissive to it; we cannot have too much confidence in that will, we cannot abandon ourselves too much to it. God's will desires and can always accomplish what will contribute most to our perfection on condition that we allow God to act. Faith does not doubt this. The more our senses are faithless, revolted, uncertain and in despair, the more surely faith says: 'This is God; all is well.'

There is nothing that faith does not penetrate and surmount. It passes beyond all darkness, and no matter how deep the shadows, it passes through them to the truth which it always firmly embraces and from which it is never separated.

§3. *The divine action offers us at each moment infinite benefits in the measure of our faith and our love*

If we are able to envisage each moment as the manifestation of the will of God, we shall find in it all that our heart can desire. For what can there be more reasonable, more perfect, more divine than the will of God? Can its infinite value increase through differences of time, place and circumstance? If you are given the secret of finding it at every moment in every event, you possess all that is most precious and worthy in your desires. What do you desire, holy souls? Do not hold back, carry your longings beyond all measures and limits, dilate your hearts to an infinite extent, I have enough to fill them: there is no moment at which I cannot make you find all that you can desire.

The present moment is always full of infinite treasure, it contains far more than you have the capacity to hold. Faith is the measure; what you find in the present moment will be according to the measure of your faith. Love also is the measure: the more your heart loves, the more it desires, and the more it desires the more it finds. The will of God presents itself at each instant like an immense ocean which the desire of your heart cannot empty, although it will receive of that ocean the measure to which it can expand itself by faith, confidence and love. The whole of the created universe cannot fill your heart which has a greater capacity than everything else that is not God. The mountains which affright your eyes are tiny as atoms to the heart. The divine will is an abyss, the opening of which is the present moment. Plunge into this abyss and you will find it ever deeper than your desires. Pay court to no one, do not worship illusions, they can neither enrich you nor deprive you of anything. The sole will of God will wholly fill you and leave you with no void; adore that will, go straight towards it, pierce through and abandon all external appearances. The stripping, death and destruction of the senses establish the reign of faith: the senses adore creatures, faith adores the divine will. Take away their idols from the senses, they weep like children in despair; but faith triumphs, for faith cannot be deprived of the will of God. When the event of the present moment terrifies, starves, strips and attacks all the senses, it is just at that moment that it nourishes, enriches and vitalizes faith, which laughs at the losses of the senses as the governor of an impregnable town laughs at useless attacks.

When the will of God has been revealed to a soul and has made it feel that God is ready to give himself completely if the soul for its part will also give itself, the soul experiences in all circumstances a powerful assistance. From now on it tastes by experience the joy of the coming of God, and it enjoys it the more the better it understands in practice the self-abandonment in which it should remain at every moment to that all-adorable will.

§4 *God reveals himself to us in the commonest events, in a manner as mysterious but as real and adorable as in the great events of history and the Sacred Scriptures*

The written word of God is full of mysteries; his word executed in action in the events of the world is no less so. These two books are truly sealed, the letter of them both kills. God is the centre of faith, and faith is an abyss of darkness which from that centre spreads itself over all the operations which proceed from it. All these words and works are, as it were, but the dark rays of a still darker sun. In vain do we open the eyes of the body to see this sun and its rays; even the eyes of our soul by which we see God and his works are but closed eyes. Here darkness takes the place of light, knowledge is ignorance, and we see without seeing. Holy Scripture is the language of a still more mysterious God; the events of the world are the obscure sayings of this same God, so hidden and so unknown. They are the drops of a great sea but of a sea of darkness. All drops, all brooks of water have the savour of their source. The fall of the angels, the fall of Adam, the impiety and idolatry of men before and after the Flood in the lifetime of the patriarchs, who knew and related to their children the story of the Creation and the then still recent preservation of the world: here are some of the dark words of Holy Scripture! A handful of men preserved from idolatry up to the arrival of the Messiah, in spite of the general loss of faith of the whole world; impiety always reigning and powerful; this little band of defenders of truth always persecuted and ill-treated; the way Jesus Christ was treated; the plagues of the Apocalypse! What! Are these the words of God? . . . Is this what he has revealed? . . . And are the effects of these terrible mysteries which last until the end of the world also the living word which teaches us his wisdom, his power, his goodness? All the events that form the history of the world express these divine attributes. All preach the same adorable word. Alas! we do not see it; we must believe it.

What does God mean by permitting the existence of Turks, protestants, all the enemies of his Church? It is all a striking lesson: it signifies the infinite perfections of God. Pharaoh and all the evil men who have followed and will follow him exist only for that purpose. Yet if we look at it, the letter of their history says the contrary; we must blind ourselves and cease to reason in order to see the divine mysteries.

Thou speakest, Lord, to all men in general by general events. Revolutions are but the tides of thy Providence which stir up storms and tempests in the minds of the inquisitive. Thou speakest in particular to all men in the events which happen to each of them from moment to moment. But instead of hearing thy voice, instead of respecting the mysterious obscurity of thy word, men see nothing but the movements of matter, blind chance and the human element; they find objections to everything; they wish to add to and subtract from thy word; they wish to reform it; they give themselves complete licence to commit excesses, the least of which would be considered by them an unheard-of crime if it were a matter of a single comma in the Holy Scriptures. For they respect the Holy Scriptures. These are the Word of God, they say, and everything contained in them is holy and true. If they do not understand their meaning they venerate them the more; they glorify and justly adore the depths of the wisdom of God. This is quite right. But what God says to you, dear souls, the words he pronounces from moment to moment, the substance of which is not paper and ink but what you suffer and what you have to do from moment to moment, does this deserve no attention from you? Why in all this do you not respect the truth and the will of God? Nothing pleases you, you criticize everything that happens. Do you not see that you are measuring by the standard of the senses and the reason what can only be measured by faith, and that reading, as you do, with the eyes of faith the word of God in Holy Scripture, you are greatly in the wrong to read it with any other eyes in his actions.

§5. *Divine action continues in our hearts the revelation commenced in Holy Scripture; but the characters in which it is written will be visible only on the Great Day*

'Jesus Christ,' says the Apostle, 'the same yesterday, today and for ever.' From the origins of the world he was, as God, the principle of the life of the just; from the first instant of his incarnation his humanity participated in this prerogative of his divinity. He works in us all through our life; the time which will elapse before the end of the world is but a day and this day is filled with him. Jesus Christ has lived in the past and still lives in the present; he began in himself and continues in his saints a life that will never finish. O life of Jesus which includes and exceeds all the ages of time, O life which is initiating new operations at every moment! . . . If the whole world is so incapable of understanding all that could be written of the individual life of Jesus, of his words and actions when he was on earth, if the Gospel gives us only the rough sketch of a few little details of it, if that first hour of his life is so unknown and so fertile, how many gospels would have to be written to recount the history of all the moments of this mystical life of Jesus Christ which multiplies wonders infinitely and eternally, since all the æons of time are, properly speaking, but the history of the divine action?

The Holy Spirit has set out for us in infallible and incontestable characters certain moments of this vast space of time. He has collected in the Scriptures certain drops, as it were, of this ocean. We see there the secret and unknown ways by which he caused Jesus Christ to appear in the world. We can follow the channels and veins of communication which in the midst of the confusion of the sons of men distinguish the origin, the race, the genealogy of this first-born child. The whole of the

Old Testament is but a sketch of the inscrutable depths of this divine work; it contains only what is necessary to find Jesus Christ. The Divine Spirit has kept all the rest hidden among the treasures of his wisdom. Of all this ocean of divine action he reveals to us but a tiny stream of water which, having reached Jesus, loses itself in the Apostles and disappears in the Apocalypse, so that the history of the divine operations, in which consists the life of Jesus in holy souls until the consummation of the ages, can only be divined by our faith.

To the manifestation of the truth of God by word has succeeded the manifestation of his charity by action. The Holy Spirit carries on the work of the Saviour. While he assists the Church in the preaching of the gospel of Jesus Christ, he writes his own gospel, and he writes it in the hearts of the faithful. All the actions, all the moments of the saints make up the gospel of the Holy Spirit. Their holy souls are the paper, their sufferings and their actions are the ink. The Holy Spirit, with his own action for pen, writes a living gospel, but it will not be readable until the day of glory when it will be taken out of the printing press of this life and published.

What a beautiful history! What a fine book the Holy Spirit is writing now! The book is in the press, there is no day on which the letters which make it up are not being composed, on which the ink is not applied and the sheets printed. But we dwell in the night of faith; the paper is blacker than the ink, the characters are all in confusion, the language is not of this world, nothing can be understood of it. You will be able to read this book only in heaven. If we could see the life of God and could contemplate all creatures, not in themselves, but in their principle, if we could also see the life of God in all objects, how his divine action moves them, mingles them, assembles them, opposes them to each other, pushes them all to the same point by diverse means, we should recognize that all things in this divine work have their reasons, their scale of measurement, their mutual relations. But how read this book the characters of which are unknown, vast in number, upside down and blotted with ink? If the blending of twenty-six letters results in such incomprehensible diversity that they suffice to compose an infinite number of different volumes, all admirable, who can express what God is doing in the universe? Who can read and comprehend the meaning of so vast a book in which there is no letter which has not its particular symbolism and does not contain profound mysteries in its tiny bulk? Mysteries cannot be seen or felt, they are objects of faith. Faith only judges of their truth and goodness by the principle on which they are delivered, for in themselves they are so obscure that their appearance does but conceal them, and blind those who would judge of them by reason alone.

Teach me, Divine Spirit, to read in this book of life! I wish to become thy disciple and like a simple child believe what I cannot see. Enough for me that my master speaks. He says so-and-so, he groups the letters of the book like this, he makes himself understood in that way; it is enough, I judge according to what he says. I do not see why, but he is the infallible truth, all that he says or does is truthful. He wills that this word should be composed of so many letters, that that word should need another number. Three, six, are enough, no others are required, one more or less would be nonsense. He alone who understands the thought can put together the letters to express it. Everything is significant; there is a perfect meaning everywhere. This line stops here because it is necessary that it should, there is not a comma missing, not a stop too many. I believe this now, and when the day of glory reveals so many mysteries to me, I shall see what at present I can only understand confusedly, and what now seems to me so complicated, so haphazard and imaginary will entrance and charm me eternally by its beauty, by the order, reason, wisdom and incomprehensible wonders that I shall find in it.

§6. *The divine action is as unworthily treated by many Christians in its daily manifestations as Jesus Christ was treated by the Jews in the days of his flesh*

What infidelity there is in the world! How unworthily do men think of God! Unceasingly we find occasions of criticizing the divine action in a way that we should not dare to criticize the least artisan in his craft. We wish to reduce God's action to the limits and rules that our feeble reason can imagine. We propose to reform it. We do nothing but complain and murmur.

We are surprised at the way the Jews treated Jesus. Ah! divine love, adorable will of God, infallible action of God, how art thou looked upon! Can the divine will intrude, can it be mistaken? But (you will say) I have this piece of business on hand, such-and-such a thing is needful to me, the necessary means for my purpose have been taken away, this man opposes me in good works. Is not this quite unreasonable? I am attacked by this illness at the moment when I cannot get on without my health.—And I tell you that the will of God is the only thing necessary and that therefore all that it does not grant is useless. No, dear souls, nothing is lacking to you; if you knew what these events which you call misfortunes, mishaps and contrarieties in which you see nothing that is not out of place and senseless, really are, you would be in extreme confusion. You would blame yourselves for your murmurings as for real blasphemies—but that does not occur to you. All that happens is nothing else than the will of God, and his adorable will is blasphemed by his children who do not recognize it.

When thou wast on earth, my Jesus, the Jews treated thee as one possessed of a devil, called thee a Samaritan, and today, although we know that thou livest for ever and ever, how do we look on thy adorable will that is always worthy of blessing and praise? Has a moment passed from the Creation till now, and will there be one from now until the day of judgement, in which the holy name of God is not worthy of praise—that name which fills all ages and all events and makes all things salutary! What, can the will of God do me harm? Shall I fear, shall I fly from the name of God; where then shall I go to find something better, if I fear God's action on me and repulse the effect of his divine will?

How ought we to listen to the word which is spoken to us in the depth of our hearts at every moment? If our senses and our reason do not understand or penetrate the truth and goodness of that word, is it not on account of their incapacity for divine truths? Should I be astonished because a mystery disconcerts my reason? God speaks: it is a mystery, i.e. it is the death of my senses and my reason, for it is the nature of mysteries to immolate them. A mystery is life to the heart through faith, but for the rest of our faculties a contradiction. The divine action kills and vitalizes with the same stroke; the more lethal it appears, the more we believe it to give life; the darker the mystery, the more light it contains. This is why a simple soul finds nothing more divine than that which in appearance is least divine. The life of faith consists entirely in this incessant battle with the senses.

§7. *Divine love gives itself to us through the medium of all creatures which communicate it to us under veils, like the Eucharistic species*

What great truths are hidden from the eyes even of Christians who think themselves very enlightened!

How few among them understand that all crosses, all actions, all spiritual impulses that are in the divine design give us God in a way that can be best explained by comparison with the most august mystery of all! Yet, what is more certain? Does not reason, as well as faith, reveal to us the real presence of the divine love in all creatures and in all the events of life as indubitably as the word of Jesus Christ and the Church reveal to us the presence of the sacred flesh of our Saviour under the Eucharistic species? Do we not know that by all these creatures and all these events, the divine Love desires to unite himself to us, that he has produced, ordained or permitted everything that surrounds us or happens to us in view of this union, the sole end of all his designs; that he uses, to attain this end, the worst as well as the best of creatures and the most disagreeable as well as the pleasantest events, and that the more naturally repellent the means of that union, the more meritorious it becomes? But if all this is true, why should not every moment of our lives be a sort of communion with divine love continuously producing in our souls the fruits of that communion in which we receive the body and blood of the Son of God? The latter, truly, has a sacramental efficacy lacking to the former, but on the other hand how much more frequently the former can be renewed and how greatly can its merit grow through the perfection of the dispositions in which it is performed. How true that the holiest life is mysterious in its simplicity and its apparently humble state. Divine banquet, perpetual festival. . . . God ever given and received under appearances of the greatest weakness and nothingness! . . . God chooses what is blameworthy to the natural judgement and what human prudence leaves on one side. Of all things God makes mysteries and sacraments of love, and gives himself to souls to the full extent of their faith through the very medium which might appear to injure them.

§8. *The revelation of the present moment is more useful because it is addressed personally to us*

We are well instructed only by the words that God speaks to us personally. It is not by reading or historical study that we become wise in the science of God; such methods alone produce but a vain, confused and self-inflating science. What instructs us is what happens to us from moment to moment; that is what forms in us that experimental knowledge which Jesus Christ willed to acquire before he taught it. This was indeed the only knowledge in which, according to the expression in the gospel, he could grow, because being God there was no degree of speculative science that he did not possess. But if this knowledge was useful to the Incarnate Word himself, for us it is absolutely necessary if we wish to speak to the heart of the persons whom God sends to us. We only know perfectly what experience has taught us through suffering and action. Experience is the school of the Holy Spirit who speaks to the heart words of life, and all that we say to others should come from this source. What we read and see only becomes divine knowledge by that fecundity, virtue and light which experience gives it. All that is the dough; leaven is needed and the salt of experience must season it. When lacking this salt we have only vague ideas, we are like dreamers who know the way to all cities and lose themselves on their road home.

We must then listen to God from moment to moment in order to be learned in the theology of virtue which is wholly practical and experimental. Set aside what is said to others, listen to what is said to you for your own use: you will find enough to exercise your faith, for this interior language of God by its very obscurity exercises, purifies and increases faith.

§9. *The revelation of the present moment is an ever freshly springing source of sanctity*

O, you who thirst, know that you have not far to go to find the source of living waters: that source springs up close to you, in the present moment; hasten, then, to approach it. These little brooks only tease our thirst, they measure parsimoniously the water they give us, it is the spring itself which is inexhaustible. If you wish to think, write and talk like apostles, prophets and saints, abandon yourselves as they did to divine inspiration.

O Unknown Love! it would seem that thy marvels are over, and that all we can do is to copy thy ancient volumes and quote thy words of the past! And we do not see that thy inexhaustible action is an infinite source of new thoughts, new sufferings, new actions, new patriarchs, new prophets, new apostles, new saints, who have no need to copy each other's lives and writings, but simply to live in a perpetual self-abandonment to thy secret operations. We hear perpetually of the 'early centuries', 'the times of the saints': what a way to talk! . . . Are not all times the successive effects of the divine operation which pours itself forth on all the instants of time, filling them, sanctifying them, supernaturalizing them all. Was there of old some now out of date way of abandoning oneself to this divine operation? Had the saints of the first days any other secret than that of becoming moment by moment what the divine action wished to make of them? And will that divine action not continue to shed its glory until the end of the world on those souls who abandon themselves to it without reserve?

Yes, dear Love, adorable, eternal, eternally fruitful and ever marvellous! Action of my God, you are my book, my doctrine, my science; in you are my thoughts, my words, my actions, my crosses. It is not by consulting your other works that I shall become what you wish to make of me, it is by accepting you in all things, in the one, ancient, royal way of my fathers. I will think, I will be enlightened and speak as they did: it is in this way that I wish to imitate, quote and copy them all.

§10. *The present moment is the manifestation of the name of God and the coming of his kingdom*

The present moment is always the ambassador who declares the order of God. The heart always pronounces its *fiat*. The soul pours itself forth by all these means into its centre and goal; it never stops, it travels by all winds; all routes and methods advance it equally on its journey to the high sea of the Infinite. Everything is a means and an instrument of holiness; everything without any exception. The 'one thing necessary' is always to be found by the soul in the present moment. There is no need to choose between prayer and silence, privacy or conversation, reading or writing, reflection or the abandonment of thought, the frequentation or avoidance of spiritual people, abundance or famine, illness or health, life or death; the 'one thing necessary' is what each moment produces by God's design. In this consists the stripping, the self-abnegation, the renunciation of the creature in order to be nothing by or for oneself, in order to remain as regards everything in God's order at his pleasure, finding one's only contentment in bearing the present moment, as if there were nothing else in the world to expect.

If everything that happens to a self-abandoned soul is 'the one thing necessary', it is evident that nothing is lacking to it and that it should never complain. If it does complain, it is wanting in faith and living by its reason or its senses, which, not seeing the sufficiency of grace, are discontented. To sanctify the name of God is, in the language of the Scriptures, to recognize his holiness, to love and adore it in all things. Things indeed proceed like words out of the mouth of God. God creates at each moment a divine thought which is signified by a created thing; thus, all those things by which he makes his will known to us are so many names and words under cover of which he shows us his desire. In itself this will is one, its name is unknown and ineffable, but it becomes multiplied to the infinite in its effects, which are, as it were, so many names that it takes. To sanctify the name of God is to know, adore and love the ineffable Being which this name expresses. It is also to know, adore and love his adorable will at every moment and in all its effects, looking at all events as so many veils, or shadows, or names of that eternally holy will. For that will is holy in al lits works, in all its words, in all its appearances, in all the names it bears.

This was how Job blessed the name of God. That complete desolation which signified for him the will of God was blessed by this holy man; he did not consider it to be ruin but one of God's names, and in blessing it, he protested that the divine will expressed under the most terrible appearances was holy, no matter what its name or form. David also blessed it in all times and places. It is then by this continual discovery, by this manifestation, this revelation of God's will in all things that his kingdom dwells in us, that he does on earth what he does in heaven, that he nourishes us without ceasing. Self-abandonment to his will includes and contains the whole substance of that incomparable prayer dictated to us by Jesus Christ. We recite it several times a day according to the orders of God and Holy Church, but we say it constantly in the depths of our heart when we love to suffer and do what is ordained for us by his adorable will. What the mouth can only pronounce syllable by syllable, word by word, taking time to do so, the heart truly pronounces at every instant, and it is thus that simple men are called to bless God in the depths of their souls. Yet they bewail their inability to praise him as they would wish, so true is it that God gives to these souls of faith his favours and graces through that very circumstance which seems to indicate their privation. It is the secret method of divine wisdom to impoverish the senses while enriching the heart, so that the latter is filled in proportion to the painful emptiness that the former experience.

What happens at each moment bears the imprint of the will of God and of his adorable name. How holy is that name! How just, then, to bless it, to treat it as a sacrament which hallows by its own power souls which place no obstacle to its action! Can we see what bears this august name without esteeming it infinitely? It is a divine manna which falls from heaven in order to give us a constant increase in grace. It is the kingdom of holiness which comes into the soul. It is the bread of angels which is eaten on earth as in heaven. There is nothing petty about our moments if they contain the kingdom of holiness and the food of angels.

Yes, Lord, may this kingdom come in my heart for my sanctification, my nourishment, my purification, to render me victorious over my enemies! How small is that precious passing moment to the eye of the common man, how great to the eye illuminated by faith! How indeed can we deem little that which is great in the eyes of our Father who reigns in heaven? All that comes from there is most excellent, for all that comes from there bears the character of its origin.

§11. *Divine action brings to all souls the most eminent sanctity: to sanctify oneself it is sufficient to abandon oneself to it*

It is from not knowing how to make use of divine action that so many Christians pass their lives anxiously pursuing a multitude of means to perfection which may be useful when ordered by the divine will but which become injurious when they interfere with the soul's simple union with God. All this multiplicity cannot give us what is to be found in the principle of every life, which is constantly present to us and which impresses on every means it employs its own individual movement and causes its unique incomparable action.

Jesus has given us a master to whom we do not listen enough. That master speaks to all hearts, and to each he speaks a word of life, the unique word for each soul; but we do not hear him well enough. We would like to know what he says to others, and we do not listen to what he says to ourselves. We do not look at things sufficiently in that supernatural mode of being which divine action gives them. We should always welcome that divine action and reply to it (as it deserves) open-heartedly, with confidence and generosity: God's action can do no harm to those who receive it thus. This immense action of God, always the same in itself from the commencement of the ages until the end, pours itself forth at every moment and gives itself in its immensity and power to the sincere soul that adores, loves it and makes it its one source of joy. You would be delighted, you say, to find an opportunity of dying for God's sake; such an action, a life passed in such a way, would please you. To lose everything, to die abandoned, to sacrifice yourself for others; you find such ideas attractive.

As for me, Lord, in everything I glorify thy action, in which I find all the happiness of martyrdom, austerities and the service of my neighbour. Thy action is sufficient for me; in whatever manner it causes me to live and die I ám content. It pleases me for its own sake apart from the means it employs and the effects it produces, because it extends to everything, it makes everything divine. Everything is heaven to me, all my moments are pure divine action, and in life as in death I wish to remain content with that.

I shall not count the hours nor the ways of thy approach, dear Love: thou wilt always be welcome. The divine action seems to have unveiled to me its immensity. I no longer move but in its infinite bosom. All that flows from it today flowed also yesterday. In reality it is the bed of the torrent of graces which flow unceasingly, it sustains them and moves them hither and thither. No longer therefore will I seek it within the narrow covers of a book, in some saint's life or some sublime idea. These are but drops of that ocean that I see pouring itself over all creatures, which are all inundated by it. They are but tiny atoms which disappear in this abyss. Nor will I seek it in spiritual writers. No longer will I beg my bread from door to door; no longer will I pay court to creatures.

Yes, Lord, I wish to live in a way that will honour thee, as the true child of an infinitely good, wise and powerful father. I wish to live as I believe, and inasmuch as this divine action is applied in all circumstances and at all times to my perfection, I wish to live on my immense revenue which cannot fail and is always present and available in the most profitable way. Can any creature's action equal that of God? And since his uncreated hand moulds everything that happens to me, shall I go and seek help from creatures who are powerless, ignorant and without affection? I should die of thirst running from fountain to fountain, from stream to stream, while here is an engulfing sea which surrounds me on all sides with its waters! Everything becomes bread to nourish me, soap to cleanse me, fire to purify me. Everything is a means of grace for my necessities. The very thing that I seek everywhere else seeks me incessantly and gives itself to me by the hand of all creatures.

O Love, must it be that this should be unknown, that thou shouldst throw thyself, as it were, at everyone's head with all thy favours, and that men should go on seeking thee in corners where they cannot find thee! What folly on their part not to breathe the open air, not to walk about the countryside, not to find water where it abounds, not to take hold of God and taste him and find his action present in everything.

You are seeking the secret of belonging to God, dear souls? There is no other than to make use of everything which God gives you. Everything leads to union with God, everything perfects you, except sin and what is outside your duty; all you have to do is to accept everything and let God act. Everything directs you, keeps you straight and carries you along. Everything is the hand of God. Earth, air and water are God's. His action is more widely extended, more present to you than the elements. It enters you by all your senses, provided you only make use of them according to his design, for you must close them in resistance to all that is not his will. There is no atom which, in penetrating you, does not make the divine action penetrate you to the marrow of your bones. All is from it and by it. These vital liquids which pour through your veins do so only by the movement which it gives them; all the variations to be found in your movements, their strength or weakness, their languor or vivacity, their life or death, are divine instruments put into operation to effect your sanctification. All your states of body become under its operation the workings of grace. All your feelings, all your thoughts, however they may arise, all come from the invisible hand of God. No created heart or spirit can teach you what this action will bring about; you will learn it by progressive experience. Your life flows ceaselessly in this unknown abyss where all you have to do is ever to love and esteem as best what is present to you, with perfect confidence in God's action which cannot of itself do you anything but good.

Yes, dear Love, all souls would reach supernatural, sublime, wonderful, inconceivable heights, if they would all be content with thy action! Yes, indeed, if we could only allow this divine hand to act, we should reach the most eminent perfection! All would reach it for it is offered to all. All we have to do is to open our mouths, as it were, and perfection will enter of itself, for there is no soul but has in thee its infinitely perfect model and the advantage of thy ceaseless working in it. If souls were faithful to it, they would all live, act and speak divinely; it would not be necessary for them to copy each other; the divine action would individualize each one of them by the most ordinary methods.

What means have I, my God, to make thy creatures appreciate what I am saying? . . . Must I resign myself to possessing so great a treasure and to seeing souls perish meanwhile in their poverty? Must I see them drying up like desert plants while I am showing them the source of living waters? Come, simple souls, you who know nothing of devotion, who have no talent, not even the elements of primary instruction, who are ignorant of the language of spirituality, who admire and wonder at the eloquence of the wise; come and I will teach you a secret way to surpass all these brilliant people, and I will place you in such easy circumstances for the attainment of perfection that you will always find it under your feet, over your head and all around you; I will unite you to God, you shall hold him by the hand while you practise the instructions which I give you. Come, then, not to *know* the map of the land of the spirit, but to *possess* it and be at home in it without fear of losing your way. Come, not to study the theory of divine grace, not to learn what it has done through the ages and is doing today, but in order to be the simple subjects of its operations. You have no need to know the words it has taught others and to repeat them cleverly; grace will give you words which will be your own.

§12. *Divine action alone can sanctify us, for God alone knows the divine exemplar of our perfection*

The divine action executes in time the ideas which the eternal wisdom has formed of all things. All things have in God their own ideas, his wisdom alone knows them. Supposing you knew all those which have nothing to do with you personally, that knowledge would be useless for your own direction. The divine action sees in the Word the idea in accordance with which you have to be formed; this idea is your exemplar. The divine action sees in the Word all that is needed by all holy souls. Holy Scripture contains a part of it and the workings of the Holy Spirit complete it according to the exemplar contained in the Word. Is it not evident that the one and only way to receive the character of this eternal idea is to make oneself a simple subject in the hands of God, and that our own efforts and intellectual speculations will be perfectly useful for the purpose? Is it not manifest that this working cannot result from our own cleverness, intelligence or subtlety, but can only follow on our passive self-abandonment to receive all from God, placing ourselves in his hand, like the liquid metal in a mould, or a canvas before the painter's brush, or the stone before the sculptor? Is it not evident that it is not the knowledge of all these divine mysteries which the will of God works throughout the ages that is the means by which God conforms us to the image conceived of us by the Word, and that our resemblance to the divine archetype can only come to us by the impression of that mysterious seal which is not made on our intelligence by the medium of our ideas, but on our will by our abandonment of it to God?

The wisdom of the simple soul consists in contenting itself with its own business, in keeping to the limits of its own path, in not overstepping its bounds. It is not curious to know God's ways of acting, being content to know his will in its own regard; it makes no effort to guess what his will may be by comparisons and conjectures, only wishing to know what each moment reveals to it by the voice of the Word heard in the depth of its own heart without asking the Bridegroom what he says to others, in such a way that from moment to moment it is unconsciously divinized by everything. That is how the Bridegroom speaks to his bride, by the very real effects of his action not scrutinized curiously but accepted with loving gratitude. Thus the spirituality of such a soul is simple, substantial, intimately informing its whole being. It is not determined to action by ideas or tumults of words which by themselves merely inflate it. People make a great use of the intellect for purposes of piety; but the intellect is hardly necessary for such purposes; it is even contrary to them. We should only make use of what God gives us to do and suffer. People abandon this divine substance (of their life) to fill their minds with the marvels wrought by God in history instead of increasing them by their own fidelity.

The marvels of these workings of God which satisfy our curiosity in our reading serve often merely to disgust us with things small in appearance, by means of which divine love would work great things in us, if we did not despise them. What fools we are! We admire and glorify God's action in the books which describe his works, and when he is ready to continue them by writing them in our hearts, we cannot keep the paper still on which he is to write, and we prevent his action by being curious to see what he is doing in us and in others.

I ask forgiveness, divine Love, for I am setting down here my own faults, and I have not yet discovered what it is to leave thee to act in me. I have not yet yielded myself up to be placed in the mould. I have frequented thy studios, I have admired thy creations, but I have not yet attained the necessary self-abandonment to receive the strokes of thy brush. But at last I have found thee, Master, Teacher, Father and my dear Love, now I will be thy disciple; I will no more frequent any school but thine. I come home like the prodigal son hungry for thy bread. I abandon the ideas which merely tend to satisfy my intellectual curiosity; I will no longer run after various masters and books; such means I will only make use of in dependence on thy divine action, not for my own satisfaction but in order to obey thee in this as in everything else that happens. I wish to confine myself to the one and only business of the present moment, to love thee, to acquit myself of my obligations and to allow thee to act.

THE STATE OF SELF-ABANDONMENT

CHAPTER ONE

THE NATURE AND EXCELLENCE OF THE STATE OF SELF-ABANDONMENT

§1. *The designs of God for the souls whom he places in this state*

There is a time when the soul lives in God and a time when God lives in the soul. What belongs to one of these periods is unsuitable for the other. When God lives in a soul, it should abandon itself completely to his Providence. When the soul lives in God, it takes trouble regularly to furnish itself with all the means that it can think of in order to attain to union with him. All its paths are marked out, its reading, its examinations of conscience; its guide is ever at its side—everything is regulated, even its times for talking. When God lives in the soul, it has nothing more of its own, it has nothing but what he gives it, who is the principle which animates it at each moment. No provisions, no route traced in advance; the soul is like a child whom one leads where one wishes, and who has nothing but feeling to distinguish what is presented to it. No books are appointed for such a soul, often enough it is deprived of a director; God leaves it without any other support than himself alone. Its dwelling-place is in darkness, forgotten and abandoned by creatures, in death and nothingness. It feels its necessities and miseries without knowing how or when it will be helped. It waits in peace and without anxiety for someone to come and help it; its eyes gaze only heavenwards. God, who can find no purer disposition in his spouse than this laying on one side of all that it is, in order to exist only by his grace and divine operation, furnishes it at the appropriate moment with books, thoughts, advice, counsels, examples and insight into its own condition. All that others find by their labours, this soul finds in its self-abandonment; and what others carefully put aside so as to find it again when necessary, a self-abandoned soul receives at the moment of need and then relinquishes it, accepting precisely from it just what God wishes to give, so as to live only by him. Others undertake an infinity of things for the glory of God; this soul often remains quietly lost in some corner like the remains of a broken pot of which no one can make any further use. There this soul remains deserted by all creatures but in the enjoyment of God through a very real, authentic and active love, although this is infused while it remains in repose. It proceeds to nothing by its own movement, all it can do is to abandon itself into God's hands, to serve him in the way that he wishes. Often it does not know what use it is, but God knows. Men think it useless and appearances are in favour of this judgement; it is, however, none the less true that from its secret resources and by hidden channels it pours an infinite number of graces on persons who are not thinking of it and of whom it does not think.

Everything in these self-abandoned souls preaches apostolically and efficaciously. God gives to their silence, their self-forgetfulness, their repose, their detachment, their words, their actions a certain virtue which works in hearts without their being conscious of it, and directed as they are by the haphazard actions of innumerable creatures of whom grace makes use for their instruction without their knowing it, they also serve others with support and guidance, without any explicit connection or intention. God works in them often by unforeseen and secret movements, so that these souls are like Jesus from whom a secret healing virtue went out to others. There is this difference, that in their case they often do not feel this virtue going out from them and even do not themselves consciously contribute to the fact. It is like a hidden balm which men do not see but of which they perceive the fragrance: a balm unconscious of its own power.

§2. *The soul in this state is led by the divine action through all obscurities*

When the soul has discovered this divine influence it leaves all its good works, its practices of devotion, its methods of prayer, its books, its ideas and consultations with spiritual people in order to be under the guidance of God alone by abandoning itself to this influence which becomes the one and only principle of its perfection. It is in his hand, as all the saints have always been, it knows that God alone knows the way that is right for it, and that if it sought for created means of action, it could do nothing but lose its way in this unknown land where God makes it walk. It is therefore his unknown action that directs and leads these souls by ways known only to him. These souls are something like the movements of the air. They can only be known in the actual present moment; what is to follow has its causes in the will of God, and his action can only be explained by its effects, by what it does in these souls and what it actually causes them to do, whether by secret, unsuspected instincts or by the duties of the state of life in which they live. This is all they know of spirituality, here are all their visions and revelations, this is all the wisdom and counsel they have, and it is of such a kind that they never lack anything. Faith assures them of the excellence of what they do: if they read, if they talk, if they ask advice, it is only to find the means of discerning the divine action. All this belongs to the order of divine action and they accept it as part of the whole, apprehending underneath these things the divine influence, while leaving on one side the things themselves. They make use of what happens to be there or what happens to be lacking, supported through faith by this infallible, even, immutable and always efficacious divine action at every moment. This action they see and enjoy in everything, in the humblest as in the greatest objects; every moment gives it them entire. Thus they make use of things with confidence, but also in submission to God's orders and his divine operation which they find with equal facility and certitude under the most contradictory appearances. Thus their lives are passed not in investigations, in desires, in disgust and in sighs, but in the continual assurance of the possession of the most perfect.

All the states that body and soul endure, all that happens to them internally and externally and that each moment reveals to them, is for them the plenitude of divine action, it is their happiness. The whole of creation is for them nothing but misery and starvation; what God's action does is the true and real measure of things. So that if his action removes their thoughts, their words, their books, their food, their friends, their health, their life itself, it is just the same as if it did the contrary. The soul loves the divine action and believes it to be equally sanctifying under all its forms. It does not reason about the way it is led, it is enough that things should come to it from this source in order to win its approval.

§3. *The state of self-abandonment includes the states of pure faith, pure hope and pure love*

The state of self-abandonment consists of a certain mingling of faith, hope and charity in one single act which unites the heart to God and his action. These three virtues united are but one virtue, they produce one single act, one single elevation of the heart to God and a simple self-abandonment to his action. How express this divine blend, this spiritual essence? How find a name which will rightly describe its nature and idea, that will enable us to conceive the unity of this trinity? It consists, in its three virtues, in one single possession and enjoyment of God and of his will. The soul sees this adorable object, it loves it and it hopes everything from it. This state might be called with equal justice pure love, pure hope and pure faith, and if the state of which we speak is usually designated by the last-mentioned name, it is not meant to exclude the other theological virtues, it is rather to make us understand that in this state those other virtues are exercised in an obscure manner.

On God's side nothing is more assured than this state; on the side of the human heart nothing is more disinterested. On God's side there is the absolute certitude of faith, and on the side of the heart certitude seasoned with fear and hope. O lovable unity in trinity of these holy virtues! Believe then, holy souls, hope and love; but do so as a result of a simple touch of your heart by the Divine Spirit which God grants you. That is the unction of the name of God with which the Holy Spirit anoints you in the depth of your heart. Behold this word and this mystical revelation, this earnest of predestination and all its happy consequences: *Quam bonus Israël Deus his qui recto sunt corde!*

This touch of the Holy Spirit in souls on fire is called pure love on account of the torrent of pleasure that pours over all their faculties with a plenitude of confidence and illumination; but in the case of souls fed on bitter herbs this touch is called pure faith, for they contain nothing but darkness and the shadows of the night. Pure love sees, feels and believes. Pure faith believes without seeing or feeling. That is the meaning of the difference in definition. It is only founded on appearances which are not identical in all cases, for in reality just as the state of pure faith is not without love, neither is the state of pure love without faith or self-abandonment; these terms are 'appropriated' to each state in virtue of their dominant factor. The different blending of these virtues under the divine touch causes the variety of all supernatural and exalted states. And inasmuch as God can blend them with infinite variety, there is no soul that does not receive his touch with personal individualizing characteristics. But what matter? The ingredients are always faith, hope and charity.

Self-abandonment is a general means for the reception of special virtues in all these various divine touches. Not all souls can aspire to receive the same kind of virtue or the same state from these divine impressions, but all can unite themselves to God, all can abandon themselves to his action, and thus all can receive the touch belonging to that state which is appropriate for them, and, finally, all can find the kingdom of God and share in its justice and its benefits. In this empire every soul can aspire to a crown, and whether it be a crown of love or a crown of faith it is always a crown, and a crown in the kingdom of God. The difference, indeed, remains that some dwell in light and some in darkness, but what does this matter so long as they are controlled by God and his action? Is it the name of the state, its specific distinction or excellence that the soul seeks? Not at all; it is God himself and his action. The *manner* of his reception should be indifferent to the soul.

Let us then preach to all souls the gospel—not of the state of pure faith or of pure love, not of the cross or of the caress; all cannot receive these in the same degree or manner—but let us preach to all simple hearts that fear God the gospel of self-abandonment to the divine action in general, and let us make them all understand that they will receive by that means the special state which has been chosen for them from all eternity. Let us not distress or reject souls or keep any away from eminent perfection. Jesus calls all the world to it since he demands that all should submit to the will of his Father and form his mystical body, the members of which cannot truthfully call him their head except in so far as their wills are perfectly attuned to his. Let us repeat unceasingly to all souls that the invitation of their sweet and loving Saviour exacts nothing of them that is difficult or extraordinary. He does not demand their labour; he desires that their goodwill should be united to him that he may lead and direct them, and favour them in proportion to the intensity of that union.

§4. *The state of self-abandonment comprises the most heroic generosity*

There is nothing more generous than a believing heart that sees only the divine life in labours and mortal dangers. If it be necessary to swallow poison, to march to the breach, to devote oneself to the service of the plague-stricken, such duties are seen to contain a plenitude of divine life, not distilled drop by drop, but in an instant inundation which swallows up the soul. An army animated by such views would be invincible. For the instinct of faith elevates and dilates the heart beyond and above all that is presented to the senses.

The life of faith is one and the same thing as the instinct of faith. It consists of joy in God's gift and a confidence founded on the expectation of his protection which makes everything harmonize and makes us receive everything with a good grace. It produces a certain indifference of soul and prepares us for all situations, all states and all persons we may meet. Faith is never unhappy, even when the senses are in a state of desolation. The soul ever maintains a living faith in God and in his action beyond the contrary appearances that darken the perceptions of the senses.

The senses suddenly cry out in terror to the soul: 'Unhappy one, now you are lost, you have no resource left!' and faith with a stronger voice replies at once: 'Keep firm, advance and fear nothing.'

§5. *The state of self-abandonment and pure faith gives the soul more merit than the most striking good works*

All the extraordinary things we see in the saints, visions, revelations, interior locutions are but external rays of the excellence of their state contained and hidden in the exercise of faith. Faith possesses all that, for it knows how to see and hear God in all that happens from moment to moment. When the state of a saint's soul bursts forth visibly, it is not to say that his faith had not already that beauty, but it is in order to show forth his virtue and draw souls to the practice of it, just as the glories of Thabor and the miracles of Jesus Christ were not, as it were, 'extras', but rather flashes of his glory which from time to time pierced the dark cloud of his humanity in order to render it venerable and lovable to others.

The true marvel of a saint is his life of continual faith through everything. If he had not that, the rest of his gifts would not make him holy. His holiness based on the loving faith which causes him to enjoy God in everything needs no exterior wonders; if such have their use it is for the sake of others who may need this testimony. As for the soul of faith contented in its obscurity, it does not rest on these brilliant manifestations; it lets them appear externally for the benefit of its neighbour, keeping for itself the most ordinary elements it can find, the order of God and his good pleasure which exercise its faith in obscurity rather than in manifestation. Faith asks for no proofs, and those who need them have less faith than those who do not. Those who live by faith do indeed receive proof, not as such but in the course of the divine order, and in this sense there is no contradiction between these extraordinary events and the state of pure faith. For there are many saints whom God raises up for the salvation of souls and from whose countenance he causes rays to proceed which enlighten the feeblest souls. Such were the Prophets and Apostles, and, indeed, such are all the saints when God chooses to place them, as it were, in a candlestick. There always will be, as there always have been, saints like these as well as an infinite number of others in the Church who are hidden, who, being intended to shine only in heaven, send forth no light in this life, but live and die in profound obscurity.

§6. *The state of self-abandonment contains the merit of all other particular spiritual operations*

Self-abandonment in the heart includes all possible ways of serving God: for one's own being is given up to the good pleasure of God, and the transport caused by pure love covers the whole field of operations of God's good pleasure. Thus the soul at every moment exercises an infinite self-abandonment and all possible qualities and manners of serving God are included in its virtue. It is not the business of the soul to determine the particular matter of the submission it owes to God, its sole business is to be ready for everything and to submit to everything. There lies the essence of self-abandonment; that is what God demands of the soul. The free self-offering that he asks of the heart consists of abnegation, obedience and love: the rest is his business. Whether the soul takes pains to fulfil the duty of its state of life, or follows with sweetness an attraction inspired by God, or peacefully submits to the impressions of grace on its body and soul is no matter: in all this it exercises in the depth of the heart one and the same general act of self-abandonment. This act is not in the least limited by the term of the soul's activity and by the special divine order which appear at the moment, but has in its depths all the merit and all the efficacy that a sincerely good will always has when the effect is outside its control. What the soul has wished to do is taken as done before God.

If the good pleasure of God sets limits to our exercise of our particular faculties, he puts none on the exercise of the will. The good pleasure of God, the being and essence of God are the object of the will, and through the soul's exercise of love God unites himself to it without limit of mode or measure. If in a particular case this love is directed in the concrete to the exercise of this or that particular faculty, it means that the will of God also directs itself to that particular object, and that God's will, as it were, foreshortens itself in the present moment, thus passing into the faculties and thence into the heart. Finding the heart pure and resigned without limit or reserve, God's will communicates itself fully on account of the heart's infinite capacity actuated by the virtue of love, which having emptied it of everything else has made it capable of receiving God.

O holy detachment! It is this that makes room for God. O purity, O blessed annihilation, O submission without reserve! This is what attracts God into the depth of the heart. Let my faculties be what they will, thou, Lord, art all my good. Do what thou wilt with this little creature: that he should act, that he should be inspired, that he should be the subject of thy impressions is all one, for all belongs to thee; all, indeed, is thee, from and for thee. I have nothing more to say to it or to do. Not a single moment of my life is of my own ordering; all belongs to thee, I have neither to add nor subtract, to inquire or reflect: sanctity, perfection, salvation, direction, mortification, is all thy affair, Lord. Mine to be content with thee and to choose for myself no action or condition, but to leave all to thy good pleasure.

§7. *All souls are called to the enjoyment of the infinite benefits of this state*

It is then self-abandonment that I preach, O God, and no particular state of life. I love all the states in which thy grace places souls without any personal preference for one over another. I teach all souls a general means of arriving at that state which thou wilt assign to them; all that I ask from them, is the will to abandon themselves to thy leading; thou wilt make them arrive infallibly at what is best for them. I preach faith to them: self-abandonment, confidence and faith; the will to be the subject and instrument of the divine action and to believe that at every moment and in all things this action is simultaneously applied according to the state of the soul's goodwill; that is the faith I preach. It is not a special state of faith and pure love, but a general state by which all souls can find God under the different ways in which he clothes himself, and can receive the divine form which his grace has prepared for them. I have already spoken to souls in distress, I am speaking now to all kinds of souls. My heart's true instinct is to belong to everyone, to announce to all the secret of the Gospel and make myself all things to all men. In this disposition of mind I consider it a duty (which I obey without difficulty) to weep with those who weep, to rejoice with those who are in joy, to talk with the simple in their own language and to make use of more learned and careful terms with *savants*. I wish to make all men see that they can aspire, not indeed to the same special favours of certain others, but to the same love, the same self-abandonment, the same God, the same work for him and consequently, all without distinction, to an eminent sanctity. What are called extraordinary and privileged graces are so called solely because there are few souls faithful enough to be worthy to receive them. This will be seen clearly on the day of judgment. It will, alas, be seen on that day that it was not in consequence of any reserve on God's part that the majority of souls were deprived of this divine largesse, but solely through their own fault. What an abundance of good would have been poured into their bosoms had they made a complete and constant submission of their goodwill to God. The same reasoning applies to the divine action as to Jesus. If those who had neither confidence in him nor respect for him did not receive the favours which he offered to everyone, they had only their own evil dispositions to thank. All, it is true, cannot aspire to the same sublime states, to the same gifts or degrees of excellence, but if all, faithful to grace, corresponded each according to his measure, all would be content because all would arrive at a point of excellence and of God's favour that would fully satisfy their desires. They would be content both in the realm of nature and that of grace, for nature and grace are indistinguishable in the sighs which the desire of this precious union with God causes to rise from the depth of the heart.

§8. *All the riches of grace are the fruit of purity of heart and of perfect self-abandonment*

He, therefore, who wishes to enjoy the abundance of all goods has but one thing to do: to purify his heart, to detach himself from creatures and abandon himself entirely to God. In this purity and this abandonment he will find everything. Let others, Lord, ask all sorts of gifts from thee, multiplying their words and their prayers; as for me, I will ask one gift only, and I have only this one prayer to make to thee. Give me a pure heart! O man of pure heart! how happy you are. You see God in your heart through the liveliness of your faith. You see him in everything and at every moment working within you and without. You are in all things his subject and his instrument. He leads you in everything and to everything. Often you do not think about it, but he thinks for you. It is sufficient that you should desire what happens, and ought to happen to you, by his command; he knows how to prepare you for it. In your salutary blindness, you hunt about to discover this desire in yourself and you cannot see it. He sees it well enough. But how simple you are! Do you not know what a well-disposed heart is? It is nothing but a heart where God is found. Seeing his own intentions in such a heart, God knows that it will always remain submissive to his orders. At the same time he knows that you do not know what is good for you and he makes it his business to give it you. He does not mind disappointing you. You thought you were going eastwards, he takes you to the west. You were on the point of striking something dangerous, he turns the rudder and brings you safe to port. Without chart or course, knowing nothing of wind or tide all your voyages are successful. If pirates cross your bow, an unexpected puff of wind takes you out of their reach.

A good will, a pure heart! How rightly did Jesus place them among the beatitudes. What greater happiness than to possess God and be possessed by him! The soul sleeps peacefully on the breast of Providence playing with the divine wisdom like an innocent child without anxiety about the journey which continues without interruption, and in spite of rocks and pirates and continual storms pursues its even way!

The pure heart, the good will; this is the sole foundation of all spiritual states! It is to it that are given the gifts of pure faith, pure hope, pure confidence and pure love. It is on this trunk that are grafted the flowers of the desert, by which I mean those precious graces which one sees blooming only in those wholly detached souls in whom God makes his habitation as in a deserted place to the exclusion of every other object. It is the fertilizing spring where rise all the streams that water the flowers of the Bridegroom and the garden of the Bride. We may imagine the pure heart addressing all souls in these terms: 'Look at me well. I am the producer of fair love, that love which discerns the better part and fixes on it; it is I who bring to birth that sweet and efficacious fear which gives the soul a horror of evil and renders it easy to avoid; to me is due the knowledge which reveals to us the greatness of God and the value of virtue; it is from me that ardent desires full of holy hope are ceaselessly springing; it is I who cause the soul to be constant in the practice of virtue in the expectation of that divine object, the enjoyment of which will one day, as now, but more perfectly, make the happiness of faithful souls.'

The pure heart can invite all souls to enrich themselves out of its inexhaustible treasures, for to the pure heart all spiritual states and methods lead back. It is from purity of heart that they draw all their beauty and charm. The wonderful fruits of grace and all sorts of virtues, so nutritious for the soul and bursting into blossom on all sides, are the results of purity of heart. This is the land flowing with milk and honey.

Come then, beloved souls, let us run, let us fly to this ocean of love that calls us. What are we waiting for? Let us start at once; let us go and lose ourselves in God, in his very heart, so as to be intoxicated with his love. We shall find in his heart the key to all heavenly treasures. Let us then take the road for heaven. No door will be shut against us, not the door of the garden, or of the cellar, or the vineyard. If we wish to enjoy the air of the country, all we need do is to go there; we shall come and go, in and out, as we will, with this key of David, this key of knowledge, this key of the abyss in which are contained the hidden and deep treasures of divine wisdom. It is also with this key that the doors of mystical death, and its sacred darkness, are opened. With it we can descend into the lakes below and the den of lions. With it souls penetrate into these obscure dungeons and return from them in safety. This key introduces us into that blessed abode where intelligence and light have their dwelling, where the Bridegroom takes his noontide repose and reveals to his faithful spouses the secrets of his love. O divine secrets which it is not lawful to reveal and which no mortal tongue can express!

Let us love then, dear souls. We need nothing but love in order to be enriched with all good things. Love gives us holiness with all its accompaniments, with both hands, so that it may flow from both sides into hearts open to these divine effusions. O divine seed of eternity, never can we sufficiently praise it. But why should we speak of it? It is better to possess it in silence than to praise it in mere words. What do I say? We must praise love, but only as a consequence of being possessed by it. For from the moment that love possesses a heart, reading, writing, talking, acting or their contraries are the same thing to it. One prefers nothing, one avoids nothing, one is a solitary, or an apostle, one is well or ill, one is rustic or eloquent—as you please. What love dictates to the heart, the heart its faithful echo repeats to the soul's other faculties. It is the heart that reigns under love's auspices over this material and spiritual composite which it is willing to take for its kingdom;

since the heart has no other instincts than those with which love inspires it, every object pleases it in the light in which love presents it. Such objects as nature or the evil spirit would fain substitute, merely disgust and horrify the heart; if God permits that it should sometimes be taken by surprise this is but to render it wiser and more humble; as soon as it recognizes its illusion, it returns to God with more love and clings to him more faithfully.

CHAPTER TWO

THE DUTIES OF SOULS WHOM GOD CALLS TO THE STATE OF SELF-ABANDONMENT

§1. *The great duty of souls whom God calls to this state is to give themselves completely and absolutely to him*

Sacrificate sacrificium justitiae et sperate in Domino: 'Offer a sacrifice of justice,' says the Prophet, 'and hope in the Lord.' This means that the great and solid foundation of the spiritual life is to give oneself to God in order to be the subject of his good pleasure in everything internal and external, and afterwards to forget oneself so completely, that one considers oneself as a thing sold and delivered to the purchaser to which one has no longer any right, in such a way that the good pleasure of God makes all our joy and that his happiness, glory and being become our sole good.

This foundation being laid, the soul has nothing to do save to pass all its life in rejoicing that God is God, abandoning itself so completely to his good pleasure, that it is equally content to do this or that, or the contrary, according to his divine will, without reflecting on the use which his good pleasure makes of it.

To abandon oneself! This then is the great duty which remains to be fulfilled after we have acquitted ourselves faithfully of the duties of our state. The perfection with which this duty is accomplished will be the measure of our sanctity.

A holy soul is but a soul freely submitted to the divine will with the help of grace. All that follows this simple acquiescence is the work of God and not of man. The soul should blindly resign itself in self-abandonment and universal indifference. This is the only disposition asked of it by God; the rest belongs to him to choose and determine according to his designs, as an architect selects and marks the stones of the building he proposes to construct.

We should then love God and his plan in everything, and we should love it as it presents itself, desiring nothing more. That these or those objects should be presented is no concern of the soul, but of God, and what he gives is best. The whole of spirituality can be expressed in abridged form in this maxim: we should abandon ourselves purely and entirely to God's design, and thus, with a complete self-forgetfulness, be eternally busied with loving and obeying him, without all these fears, reflections, twistings and turnings and disquietudes which sometimes result from the care of our own salvation and perfection. Since God offers to manage our affairs for us, let us once for all hand them over to his infinite wisdom, in order to occupy ourselves only with himself and what belongs to him.

Come, my soul, let us pass with head erect over all that happens within us or outside us, remaining always content with God, content with what he does with us and with what he makes us do. Let us be very careful not to engage imprudently in that multitude of restless reflections which like so many paths leading nowhere present themselves to our mind to make it wander and stray endlessly to our sheer loss: let us pass this labyrinth of our own self-love by vaulting over it and not by following it out in all its interminable details.

Come, my soul, let us pass beyond our languors, our illnesses, our aridities, our inequalities of humour, our weaknesses of mind, the snares of the devil and of men with their suspicions, jealousies, sinister ideas and prejudices. Let us fly like the eagle above all these clouds, our gaze ever fixed on the sun and on its rays, which are our duties. We feel all these miseries, and it is not in our power to be insensible to them, but let us remember that our life is not a life of feeling. Let us live in that higher region of the soul where the will of God produces his eternal operation, ever equal, ever uniform, ever immutable. In that spiritual home where the Uncreated, the Formless, the Ineffable, keeps the soul infinitely removed from all the shadows and dust of earth, we remain calm even when our senses are the prey of the tempest. We have become independent of the senses; their agitations and disquietudes, their comings and goings and the hundreds of metamorphoses they pass through do not trouble us any more than the clouds that darken the sky for a moment and disappear. We know that everything happens in the senses as in the air where all is without sequence or order, in a state of perpetual change. God and his will is the eternal object which charms the heart in the state of faith, as in the state of glory he will be its true felicity; and the state of the heart in glory will have its effect on the whole of our material being, at present the prey of monsters, owls and wild beasts. Under these appearances, however terrible they may be, the divine action will give to our being a heavenly power and make it as shining as the sun; for the faculties of the sensitive soul and of the body are prepared here below like gold, iron, fine linen and precious stones. Like the material substrate of those various things, they will only enjoy the splendour and purity of their form after much manipulation and when much has been destroyed and cut away. All that souls endure here below under the hand of God has no other purpose than to prepare them for this.

The soul of faith, knowing God's secret, remains ever in peace. All that happens to it, far from frightening it, reassures it. So intimately persuaded is it of God's guidance that it takes everything as a grace and forgets the instrument with which God works in order to think only of the task committed to its care. Its love stimulates it ceaselessly to fulfil faithfully and exactly its obligations. All that is distinctly perceived by a self-abandoned soul is the action of grace, with the exception of the sins which are trifling and which the action of grace turns to its advantage. I call 'distinctly perceived' all the afflicting or consoling impressions which the sensitive soul receives from the objects with which the divine will ceaselessly places it in contact for its good —'distinctly' because that is what is most clearly discerned in all that occurs to it. In all these things, faith sees only God and applies itself solely to conformity with his will.

§2. *To arrive at the state of self-abandonment, the soul must strip itself of all created things*

This state presents nothing but sweetness when attained, but many agonies have to be passed through on the road. The doctrine of pure love can only be learnt by God's action, not by any effort of our own spirit. God instructs the heart not by means of ideas, but by pains and contradictions. The science of this state is a practical knowledge by which one tastes God as the sole good. In order to possess it, we have to be disentangled from all particular goods, and to reach that state of disentanglement we have to be really deprived of them. Thus, it is only through a continual self-contradiction and a long series of all kinds of mortifications, trials and strippings that one can be established in the state of pure love. We have to arrive at the point at which the whole created universe no longer exists for us, and God is everything. For that purpose it is necessary that God should oppose himself to all the particular affections of the soul, so that when it is led to some particular form of prayer or idea of piety or method of devotion, when it proposes to attain perfection by such and such plans or ways or by the direction of such and such people, in fact, when it attaches itself to anything whatever, God upsets its ideas and permits that instead of what it thought it would do, it finds in it all nothing but confusion, trouble, emptiness, folly. No sooner has it said: that is my path, there is the person I ought to consult, that is how I should act, than God immediately says the contrary and withdraws his power from the means chosen by the soul. So, finding in everything only deception and nothingness, the soul is constrained to have recourse to God himself and be content with him.

Happy the soul that understands this loving severity of its God and corresponds to it faithfully! It rises above all that is transitory to rest in the unchangeable and infinite. It no longer lets itself go forth by love and confidence to created things, it admits them only by duty, by the command of God and a special application of his will. It lives above the alternations of abundance and deprivation in the plenitude of God who is its permanent good. God finds such a soul quite empty of individual inclinations, movements or choice. It is dead and buried in a universal indifference. The Allness of the Divine Being thus appearing in the depth of the heart spreads over the surface of creatures a tint of nothingness which absorbs all their distinctions and variety. Creatures by themselves are without power or efficacy and the heart lacks any tendency or inclination towards them because the majesty of God fills all its capacity. A heart that thus lives for God is dead to everything else and everything is dead to it. It is for God who gives life to everything to vivify the soul and other creatures in regard to it. This life is God's design. By this design the heart is moved towards creatures in so far as that is necessary or useful, and by the same design creatures are presented to the soul and accepted by it. Without this divine power of the good pleasure of God, creatures are not admitted by the soul, and the soul does not move towards them. This reduction of all creatures, first into nothing and then into the particular point of God's design, results in God being God as well as all things to the soul at each moment. For each moment is for the soul a contentment with God alone in the depth of the heart and a self-abandonment without reserve to all possible creatures, or rather to the whole created or possible universe according to the order of God. Thus each moment contains the whole.

§3. *The active exercise of self-abandonment with reference to the precepts and inspiration*

Although souls raised by God to the state of self-abandonment are much more passive than active, they cannot be dispensed from all action. This state, being nothing else than the virtue of self-abandonment practised more habitually and with greater perfection, should consist, like that virtue, of two orders of duties: the active accomplishment of the divine will and the passive acceptance of all that it pleases God to send us.

It consists essentially, we have said, in the complete donation of our being to God to be used according to his good pleasure. Now the good pleasure of God makes use of our being in two ways: he either obliges us to perform certain actions, or he simply acts himself in us. We thus have two ways of submitting to him; the faithful execution of his clearly manifested commands, and the simple and passive submission to the effects he produces in the soul, whether agreeable or painful. Self-abandonment includes all that, for it is nothing but a perfect submission to God's design according to the disposition of the present moment. It is of small importance to the soul to know in what it has to abandon itself and what the present moment may present, but it is absolutely important that it should abandon itself.

There are therefore duties of precept that must be accomplished and duties of necessity that must be accepted; and there is also a third kind of duty which also belongs to active fidelity though not concerned with actual precepts: the duties of inspiration to which the spirit of God inclines hearts that are submissive to him.

The accomplishment of this class of duties demands a great deal of simplicity, of gentle and cordial facility, of a certain sensitive mobility of the soul under the breath of grace directing it, for nothing is actually performed; one merely lets oneself go, and freely and simply obeys one's impressions. That souls may not be deceived in this way, God never fails to give them wise directors who point out the degree of liberty or reserve with which these inspirations should be utilized. This third class of duties is quite beyond and outside any law, form, or determined matter. Hence comes the individual and extraordinary element in the lives of the saints, regulating their vocal prayer, their interior communications, their feelings and the astounding quality of their life, their austerities, their zeal, their prodigality of self-sacrifice for their neighbour. Since the whole of this domain is under the interior law of the Holy Spirit, no one should advance to it or take its duties upon himself or desire it or repine because he does not receive the graces which would make him undertake this kind of good work and practise these uncommon virtues, for their real merit comes from their being in God's design. Unless we practise this reserve we shall fall under the influence of our own will and be exposed to illusion.

We should note that there are souls whom God wishes to keep hidden, little in their own eyes and those of others. Far from bestowing striking qualities on them, his design for them prescribes obscurity. They would deceive themselves if they tried to walk by any other path. If they are sufficiently instructed, they will know that their part is fidelity in their own nothingness, and their lowliness will be their peace. The only real difference between their path and the path of those who seem to be more favoured is whatever difference there may be in their love and their submission to the will of God, for if they surpass in this respect souls who seem to accomplish more in exterior works, no doubt their holiness will be greater.

This shows that every soul should content itself with the duties of its state and the commands of Providence; it is evident that God demands this equally of all. As for the attractions and the impressions the soul may receive in itself, it belongs to God alone to give them. One should not oneself try to produce them or make efforts to increase them. The effort of nature is here directly opposed and contrary to the infusion of grace. The latter comes in peace. It is the voice of the Bridegroom that should awaken the spouse, who should act only in so far as she is animated by the Holy Spirit, for in acting apart from that influence the soul accomplishes nothing. When then it feels no inclination or power of grace to imitate the marvels that make the saints so wonderful, it must judge itself and say: That is what God wants from the saints; he does not want it from me.

§4 *The conduct of the soul that is raised to the state of self-abandonment in relation to this double manifestation of the good pleasure of God*

The souls who are called by God to live in the state of perfect self-abandonment lead on earth a life like to that of Jesus, the Blessed Virgin and St Joseph. This life is entirely filled with the will of God. These souls fully submissive to the divine will as soon as it is manifested in precept or inspiration, are in continual dependence on what we may call the will of pure Providence. It follows from this that their life, though most extraordinary in its perfection, shows nothing exteriorly except what is quite ordinary and common: they fulfil the duties of religion and of their state; others apparently do the same. Examine them in other matters; there is nothing striking or peculiar; only ordinary things happen to them. What distinguishes them is not perceptible to the senses; it is the dependence on the supreme will in which they live which seems to arrange everything for them. This will keeps them always masters of themselves through the habitual submission of their hearts.

Thus the souls of whom we speak are by their state solitary and free, disengaged from everything in order to content themselves in peacefully loving the God who possesses them and faithfully fulfilling the duty of the moment according as his will is signified to them without permitting any reflection on themselves or any scrutiny of consequences, causes or reasons; it must suffice them to walk simply in pure duty as if there were nothing in the world but God and the particular duty of the moment.

The present moment is, as it were, a desert in which the simple soul sees nothing but God only, whom it enjoys, being solely occupied with his will for it; all else is left aside, forgotten, abandoned to Providence. The soul like an instrument in God's hand only accepts or does things in so far as it is passively occupied with God or directed by him to some external purpose.

This interior application of the soul is accompanied by a co-operation, free and active, indeed, but infused and mystical, which means that God, finding everything in the soul ready for action, should he ordain it, spares it the trouble, enriching it with what would have otherwise been the fruits of its own efforts and goodwill. As if someone, seeing a friend ready to make a journey for his service, were promptly to insinuate himself into his friend's person and under his friend's appearance make the journey by his own activity, so that nothing was left to the friend but his will to go, while in fact he would be walking by the other's power. His action would be free because it would be a result of a free decision taken beforehand through love for the friend who would actually perform the task; it would be active, for the journey would really be taken; it would be infused because it would take place without the friend's own action; finally, it would be mystical, for the source of the movement would be hidden.

But to return to this kind of co-operation which we have explained by this imaginary journey, it should be noted that it is totally different from the fidelity with which one fulfils one's ordinary duties. The action with which one fulfils these is neither mystical nor infused but free and active in the ordinary meaning of the words. Thus self-abandonment to God's good pleasure has in it both passivity and activity; the subject of the act makes no contribution of his own beyond the habit of general goodwill ready for anything and wishing for nothing in particular, like an instrument without any action of its own. Once it is in the workman's hands, it serves for all the uses for which its nature and quality adapt it. Contrariwise, the obedience paid to the signified and declared will of God is part of the common order of vigilance, care, attention, prudence and discretion, according as grace helps or stimulates our ordinary spiritual efforts. We leave everything else then to God's action, retaining in our own power nothing but our acts of love and obedience to the present duty, for the soul will practise these acts eternally.

This love of the soul silently infused is a true action of which it makes a perpetual obligation; it must constantly preserve it, which it cannot do without action. Such action, however, is altogether different from the obedience to the duty of the present moment by which the soul disposes its external faculties to execute completely the external will of God without expecting any extraordinary call.

The will of God is in all things the rule, the method, the law, the simple and certain way for this soul. It is the invariable law, belonging to all times, all places, all states. It is a straight line which the soul follows with courage and fidelity, straying neither to the right nor to the left and unconcerned with what exceeds its grasp: all that is beyond, is received and performed in self-abandonment. In one word, the soul is active as far as it is concerned with its present duty, but passive and abandoned as regards all the rest, where its only action is to await in peace the divine motion.

§5. *The soul that wishes to be united to God should esteem all the operations of his grace but should attach itself, for its part, to the duty of the present moment only*

It is by union with his will that one enjoys and possesses God, and it is an illusion to seek for that enjoyment by any other means. The will of God is the universal means. This means does not belong to this or that method, but it has the virtue of sanctifying all methods and special calls.

The divine will unites itself with our souls in a thousand different ways, and the method that it adopts in our regard is always the best for us. We should esteem and love them all, for in all we should see the divine design accommodating itself to each soul and choosing the best way to effect the divine union in it. The duty of the soul is to be faithful to that choice, but nevertheless to love and esteem the adorable will of God as indicated for others. For example, if the divine will prescribes for me vocal prayers, affective sentiments, illuminations on the mysteries, I shall love and esteem the silence and spiritual nudity which the view of sheer faith brings about in others, while for my own part I shall make use of this present duty and unite myself to God by means of it. I shall not reduce all religion (as the Quietists do) to complete inactivity, for what makes perfection is the order of God which renders useful to a soul any means that he chooses to apply to it. No, I will not confine the will of God to any limits or figures, but I will receive his will under the forms it may choose to adopt, and I shall think highly of those which God adopts for union with others.

Thus all simple souls have one general way differentiated and particularized in each of them so as to make up the variety of the mystical robe of the Church. All simple souls approve and esteem each other, saying: let us go each by our own path to the common goal, united in that same purpose and by the same means according to the designs of God so variously expressed in us all. This is the spirit in which we should read lives of saints and spiritual books without giving way to delusions and leaving our appointed path. This is why it is so necessary only to read and have spiritual conversations in conformity with God's design, for if they come to us as our present duty in that design, the soul far from being deceived will be confirmed in its own way both by what resembles that design and by what differs from it. But if our spiritual reading or conversation is not our present duty in the order of God for us, we shall always be troubled afterwards with a confusion of continually varying ideas, because, apart from the order of God, there can be no order anywhere.

How long shall we go on filling our receptive souls with troubles and anxieties which have nothing to do with our present duties? When will God be to us everything in all things? Let us leave creatures to produce on us impressions according to their nature, but let nothing make us halt; let us go beyond the whole of creation, and live purely on God himself.

§6. *God exacts from souls whom he places in this state the most perfect docility to the action of his grace*

How detached from everything that one feels or does must one be in order to walk by this path in which one lives on God only and one's present duty. We must cut off all more distant views, we must confine ourselves to the duty of the present moment without thinking of what preceded it or what will follow it.

I assume, of course, that the law of God is well kept and that the practice of self-abandonment has made your soul docile to divine action. You will have a feeling that will cause you to say: I feel at present an affection for this person or book, I would like to give or receive this piece of advice, to make such or such a complaint, to open myself to this soul or receive confidences, to give or do this thing or the other. You should follow this impulse under the motion of grace without relying an instant on your own reflections, reasonings or efforts. We must apply ourselves to things for the time that God wishes without mixing ourselves up in them personally. The will of God is applied to us in the state of which we are speaking; it should completely take the place of all our ordinary supports.

Each moment has its obligatory virtue to which the self-abandoned soul is faithful, yet it misses nothing of what it reads or hears; the most mortified novice does not fulfil her duties better; that is why these souls are now led to one book and now to another, or to make this or that remark on some trifling event. God gives them at one moment the desire to instruct themselves in what at another moment will help their practice of virtue.

In all that they do, they feel only the attraction of the act without knowing why. All they can say reduces to this: I feel drawn to write, to read, to ask this question, to look at that object; I follow this inclination, and God who gives it me makes in my soul a reserve-fund of such things to be in the future the means of further attractions which will enable me to make use of them in my own interest and that of others. This is what obliges such souls to be simple, gentle, flexible and mobile under the slightest, almost imperceptible, impressions of the divine will.

In the state of self-abandonment the sole rule is the present moment. The soul is as light as a feather, as fluid as water, simple as a child, as easily moved as a ball, so as to receive and follow all the impressions of grace. Self-abandoned souls have no more hardness or resistance than molten metal. For just as metal takes all the shapes of the mould into which it is poured, these souls adapt and adjust themselves as easily to all the forms which God wishes to give them. In a word, their disposition resembles that of the air which is at the service of all who breathe it and of water which takes the form of every container.

They present themselves to God like a perfectly plain and simple canvas, without concerning themselves to know the subject which it may please God to paint in their souls, for they trust themselves to him; they surrender themselves and, wholly occupied with their duty, think neither of themselves nor of what is necessary for them, nor of how they are to procure it.

The more, however, they apply themselves to their little job, so simple, so hidden, so contemptible (as its outward appearance may be), the more God diversifies and beautifies it. On the background of simple love and obedience, his hands love to trace the most beautiful details, the most delicate and exquisite drawings, the most divine figures: *Mirificavit Dominus Sanctum suum.* A canvas which is simply blindly abandoned to the painter's brush merely feels each moment the touch of the brush. Similarly if a stone could feel, it would feel nothing but the cruel edge of the chisel cutting it away and destroying it, for the stone being chipped by repeated blows is totally unaware of the figure which is being carved out of it by these blows. It feels only a chisel which is reducing it in size, is beating it, cutting it and changing its shape. Take for instance a poor bit of stone which you wish to make into a crucifix or a statue, although the stone does not know it. Suppose you ask it, 'What is happening to you?' It might answer, 'Don't ask me. As far as I am concerned there is nothing for me to know or do except to remain steady under the hand of my master, to love this master and to put up with his treatment. As for what I am destined to be, it is his business to know how to manage that. I do not know what he is doing or what I am being turned into by his work; I only know that whatever he is doing is best and most perfect, and I accept each blow of the chisel as the most excellent thing for me, although to speak the truth every blow makes me feel that I am being ruined, defaced and destroyed. But I leave all this to him and content myself with the present moment, thinking only of my duty; and I accept this skilful master's treatment of me without knowing or troubling myself about it.'

Yes, dear souls, simple souls, leave to God what belongs to him and remain loving and passive under action. Hold for certain that what happens to you internally and externally is for the best. Leave God to act and abandon yourselves to him. Let the point of the knife and the needle work. Let the brush of the master cover you with a variety of colours which seem only to disfigure the canvas of your soul. Correspond with all these divine operations by the uniform and simple disposition of a complete self-abandonment, self-forgetfulness and application to your duty. Keep to the line of your own advance and, without knowing the map of the country or the details, names and directions of the land you are passing through, walk blindly along that line and everything will be indicated to you if you remain passive. Seek only the kingdom of God and his justice in love and obedience and all the rest will be given you.

One sees many souls who are disturbed and ask: Who will give us holiness, perfection, mortification, direction? Let them hunt up in books the precise term and quantities of this wonderful business, its nature and parts; as for you, remain in peace in the unity of God by your love and walk blindly in the clear straight path of your obligations. The angels are at your side in this night and their hands make a barrier for you. If God wishes more from you, his inspiration will make it known to you.

§7. *The docility of the soul in this state should make it close its eyes on the road by which God leads it*

When God becomes the guide of a soul he demands with justice that it should confide absolutely in him and be not at all disturbed by the way in which he leads it. The soul is pushed along without seeing the road over which it is passing. What it has seen or read is no guide to it now. In the case of its own action, it must walk guided by experience; it cannot do otherwise; it cannot take risks. But divine action is always novel, it does not return on its steps, it always finds new paths. Souls led by divine action know not where they go, the paths they follow are not to be found in books or in their own reflections, divine action continually shows them the forward path; they follow it by a divine impulse.

When one is being led by night across fields, through an unknown roadless country by a guide who follows his own ideas without asking the way of anyone and without revealing his plans, what can one do but abandon oneself to his care? What is the use of trying to find out where one is, of asking the passers-by or of looking at the map? The intentions and the caprice, so to speak, of a guide who insists on our trusting him will be contrary to all that. He will take pleasure in confounding the soul's anxiety and suspicions. He demands a complete confidence in himself. If one had proof that his guidance was right there would be neither faith nor self-abandonment.

The divine action is essentially good, it needs neither reform nor control. It commenced at the moment of the Creation and up to this moment it has brought forth novelties, its operations have no limits, its fecundity is never exhausted. This was done yesterday, something else is done today; the same action which is applied at all moments produces constantly new effects, and its manifestations will go on eternally. Divine action made an Abel, a Noah, an Abraham in different patterns; Isaac is an original figure, Jacob is not a copy of him, nor is Joseph a copy of Jacob. Moses is like none of his forebears. David and the prophets are quite different to the patriarchs. John the Baptist surpasses them all. Jesus Christ is the First-born; the Apostles act more by the influence of his spirit than by a literal imitation of his works.

Jesus Christ did not limit his own action. he did not obey literally all his own maxims. The Divine

Spirit perpetually inspired his holy soul; having always been abandoned to that divine Breath there was no need to consult the preceding moment in order to determine the following one. The breath of grace formed all his moments on the model of the eternal truths which the invisible and impenetrable wisdom of the Holy Trinity preserved. The soul of Jesus Christ received the divine orders at each instant and reproduced them in his conduct. The Gospel shows us the result of these truths in the life of Jesus Christ, and the very same Jesus always living and working produces new wonders in holy souls.

Do you wish to live according to the Gospel? Live in a pure and complete self-abandonment to the action of God. Jesus Christ is the sovereign organ of that action. He was yesterday, he still is today, continuing his life, not beginning it over again. What has been done is done, what remains to be done is being done at every moment. Each saint receives a part of that divine life; Jesus Christ, though the same, is different in all. The life of every saint is the life of Jesus Christ, it is a new gospel. The cheeks of the Spouse are compared to a bed of sweet-smelling flowers. The divine action is the gardener who admirably diversifies their arrangement. This flower-bed is unlike that one; among all the flowers there are not two that resemble each other, except by the fidelity with which they receive the action of the Creator, leaving him to do what he wills as master and for their part obeying the laws he has imposed on their nature. To let God do what he wills and to do what he demands of us, that is the gospel, the whole of Scripture and the ordinary law.

§8. *This complete self-abandonment is as simple a thing as its effects are wonderful*

Such then is the straight high road of sanctity, such is the state of perfection, such are the duties it imposes, such is the great, the incomparable secret of self-abandonment, but it is a secret without a secret, an art without art. God who demands it of everyone has explained it very clearly and made it very intelligible and simple. The obscurity of the road of pure faith is not in anything that the soul has to practise, for nothing is easier and clearer to understand; the mystery resides entirely in God's action.

See what happens in the Eucharist. What is necessary in order to change the bread into the body of Jesus Christ is so simple and easy that the most ignorant priest can do it, and yet it is the mystery of mysteries in which everything is so hidden, obscure and incomprehensible, that the more spiritual and enlightened one is, the more faith one requires to believe it. The road of pure faith shows us something similar. Its effect is to make us find God at every moment; what can be more marvellous, more mystical, more beatifying! It is indeed an inexhaustible fount of thoughts, discourses and writings. It is an assemblage and a source of all marvels. And yet what is necessary for the production of this prodigious effect? One thing only. To allow God to act and to do what he wishes according to one's state of life. Nothing easier in the spiritual life or better adapted to the powers of all and yet nothing more wonderful, no path more dark. To walk in it, the soul needs a great faith; everything is suspect, reason finds difficulties everywhere. All the soul's ideas are confounded, here is nothing that it has seen or read about, nothing of what it has been accustomed to admire. The prophets were saints; this Jesus is an enchanter said the Jews. How little faith has the soul that, following their example, is scandalized, and how it deserves to be deprived of the wonders God is ready to work in it!

CHAPTER THREE

TRIALS ACCOMPANYING THE STATE OF SELF-ABANDONMENT

§1. *First trial: The blame and criticism of persons who are reputed wise and pious*

Nothing is more secure than the way of self-abandonment, just as nothing is clearer, easier or more pleasant and less exposed to possible error and illusion. Travelling on this road, we love God, we fulfil our Christian duties, we frequent the sacraments, we produce the external religious acts obligatory for everyone, we obey our superiors, we continually resist the movements of the flesh and the devil, for no one is more attentive or vigilant in fulfilling all their obligations than those who walk in this way.

If this be so, how then comes it that these souls are so often exposed to contradictions? One of their most ordinary trials is that when they have performed like other Christians the duties laid down by the strictest doctors, people try to oblige them in addition to wearisome practices which the Church does not impose, and if they make no use of them they are taxed with illusion. But tell me, is a Christian who confines himself to the observance of the commandments of God and the Church, and who without meditation or contemplation, without spiritual reading or any particular private devotion spends his time in worldly business, in error? No one thinks of charging him with it or suspecting him of it. Let us be consistent. If we leave undisturbed the Christian of whom I have just spoken it is only justice not to disquiet a soul who not only fulfils the precepts at least as well as he does, but who in addition practises external works of piety of which the former knows nothing or towards which, if he does know them, he shows nothing but indifference.

Prejudice reaches the point of assuring us that such a soul is deluded because after having submitted to all that the Church prescribes, it keeps itself at liberty to give itself up without obstacle to the intimate operations of God and follow the impressions of his grace at all moments when it has no express obligation to fulfil. It is condemned, in a word, because it spends in loving God the time that others give to recreation or worldly affairs: is not this a crying injustice? One cannot insist too strongly on this point. In the case of one who remains in the ranks and confesses once a year, nothing is said about him, he is left in peace, being perhaps occasionally exhorted to do something more but without being strongly pressed and certainly without its being put to him as an obligation. If he changes his life and comes out of the indevout multitude, at once he is attacked with maxims, methods of direction, methods of prayer, and unless he binds himself to what has been established by the art of piety and constantly follows it, he is done for, people are anxious about him and his way of life becomes suspect. Are these critics ignorant that these practices, however good and holy they may be, are, after all, only the road leading to divine union? Do they wish those who have reached the goal to stay in the road?

That, however, is what is demanded of this soul on behalf of whom these critics are so afraid of illusion. This soul has accomplished its journey like others; at the beginning it learned these practices of devotion and followed them faithfully; it would be in vain to try and keep it subject to them today. Since God, touched by the efforts that it has made to advance by means of such help, has come to meet it and has led it to this blessed union; since it has arrived in that fair region of which the atmosphere is self-abandonment and where the possession of God in love is initiated; since finally this God of goodness has substituted for its care and labour *himself* as the principle of its operations, these methods have lost their utility for it, they do but indicate the road it has passed over and left behind it. To demand that it should take up these methods again or continue to follow them would be to make it abandon the goal at which it has arrived in order to return to the road which brought it there.

Moreover, it would be a loss of time and trouble, for if this soul has any experience it will remain untroubled and unshaken in that intimate peace in which it exercises its love so advantageously. That is the centre where it will repose, or, if you wish, that is the straight line traced by God himself which it will always follow. It will walk with constancy along that line and all its duties will be marked out for it moment by moment. Following the order of that line, it will fulfil its duties without hurry or confusion as they are presented to it. For all the rest, it will remain in perfect liberty of mind, always ready to obey the movements of grace as soon as they make themselves felt, and to abandon itself to the care of Providence.

God tells it that he intends to be its master and to direct it in his own way, and he makes it understand that it cannot without infringing the sovereign rights of its Creator allow its own liberty to be enchained. It sees that if it were to confine itself within the regulations of souls who live under a regime of effort and industry, far from following the invitation of grace, it would deprive itself of a thousand things necessary for its future duties. But as people are ignorant of that, they judge it and blame its simplicity, and it who blames no one, who approves all states of life, who knows so well how to judge different degrees of progress, sees itself despised by these false sages who cannot appreciate this gentle and cordial submission to Providence.

The wisdom of the world does not approve the constant instability of the Apostles who could not fix themselves anywhere. No more can the common run of religious people endure souls who depend upon Providence in this way for their principle of movement; only a few souls of that order will approve them, and God who uses men for the instruction of men will not fail to make souls that are simple and faithful to their self-abandonment come across them.

Moreover, these souls have less need of direction than others, for they have only reached this stage with the air of very great and excellent directors. If they find themselves momentarily left to themselves, it is but by the disposition of Providence when death takes, or some event places at a distance, the guides who had introduced them into this state. Even in these circumstances they are always disposed to accept direction, only they peacefully await the moment of Providence. And then without fussing about it, from time to time they will meet persons in whom, without knowing them or where they come from, they will feel a secret confidence at such times of privation. Such a feeling is a sign that God wishes to make use of them at the moment to communicate some lights. These souls then consult and follow with complete docility the advice they receive, but if this help does not present itself they cling to the maxims given them by their first directors. They are thus always being truly directed either by the original principles which they imbibed heretofore or by these chance counsellors, and they make use of them until God sends them persons in whom they can confide and who reveal his will to them.

§2. *Second trial in the state of self-abandonment: The apparent uselessness and external defects which are the portion of souls whom God wishes to raise to this state*

A second trial of souls whom God leads by this way results from their apparent uselessness and their external defects. As a rule, neither honours nor revenues come their way, but rather a state of life abject and useless from the world's point of view. No doubt, those who occupy important posts are not on that account necessarily excluded from the state of self-abandonment, and even less is this state incompatible with the shining virtues of a sanctity which imposes universal veneration. But how much more numerous are the souls raised to this sublime state whose virtues are known to God only. Such souls are by their state freed from almost all exterior obligations. They are hardly fitted for the world, for business or for industrial occupations, for complicated situations or for study. They seem useless for anything, the only noticeable thing about them is their weakness of body, mind, imagination and passions. They pay attention to nothing. Their life is, so to speak, a brute-life; one sees in them none of the advantages which culture, study and reflection bring to men. Their nature seems like that of children before they are placed in the hands of educators to be formed. Their defects are obvious, and, though these do not make them more guilty than children, they are more shocking in them. God takes everything from these souls but innocence, so that they may possess nothing but himself alone.

The world, which does not understand this mystery,

judges by appearances only and finds nothing to appreciate or esteem. So the world rebuffs and despises them, they are indeed butts for everyone's censure. The nearer one sees them the less one likes them, in fact the more one dislikes them: one does not know what to say or think of them. Nevertheless, something or other seems to speak in their favour, but instead of following that instinctive feeling, or at least of suspending one's judgement, we prefer to follow the leading of our malignity. People spy on their actions so as to confirm their own opinion, and like the Pharisees who could not endure the conversation of Jesus, scrutinize them with such prejudiced eyes that all they do seems ridiculous or criminal.

§3. *Third trial: Interior humiliations*

Contemptible in the eyes of others, the souls whom God raises to this state are still more so in their own. There is nothing about their sufferings or actions but what is very trivial and humiliating, there is nothing striking about their manner of life, all about them is commonplace. Within are nothing but troubles, without nothing but contradictions and plans that fail, and a sickly body needing care and comforts which seem to be the opposite of the excesses of poverty and austerity which have made us admire the saints. In the case of these souls we see neither heroic enterprises nor excessive fasts or alms-giving, nor ardent and heroic zeal.

Simply united to God by faith and love, they see all their interior feelings in disorder. They despise themselves still more when they compare themselves with those who pass for saints, and who, capable as they are of subjection to rules and methods, show nothing but what is correct in public opinion in all their person and actions. Then the sight of themselves is insupportable and covers them with confusion. This is what draws from their hearts those sighs and bitter groanings which mark the excess of grief and affliction with which they are filled. Let us remember that Jesus Christ was at once God and Man. As Man he was reduced to nothingness and as God was filled with glory. These souls without sharing his glory feel nothing but the death and annihilation caused in them by their sad and grievous appearance. They appear, to the eyes of men, as Jesus did to Herod and his court.

As regards their senses and judgement, these poor souls are thus led in a way that is altogether disgusting to them, for none of all this is pleasant to them; they long for something quite different, but all the roads leading to that sanctity they so desire are closed to them. They have to live on this bread of ashes and anguish under continual external and internal constraint. It is their lot to perceive an ideal of sanctity which causes them constant and irremediable torments. Their will is famished for it, but they have no means of effectively attaining it. Why all this, if not in order that the soul should be mortified in its most intimate and spiritual part, and finding no satisfaction or happiness in anything that happens to it should place all its happiness in God who is leading it expressly by that way, so that there should be none but himself who can be its pleasure?

I think that the conclusion from all this is easy, that these abandoned souls cannot, like others, occupy themselves with desires, pursuits, and matters of detail, that they cannot combine with other people, enter into plans or prescribe for themselves methodical ways or detailed plans for action or reading. If they could, it would imply that they were still in a position to dispose of themselves and this is excluded by the state of self-abandonment in which they are. In that state one belongs to God by a full and complete cession of all one's rights over oneself, over one's actions, one's thoughts, one's movements, over the employment of one's time and over all one's relationships. One only desire remains to be fulfilled; to keep one's eye on the Master to whom one has given oneself and to be constantly on the alert to divine his will and execute it immediately. No condition better represents this state than that of a servant who is in his master's presence only to obey at each instant the orders he may please to give him and not to conduct his own affairs, which he should abandon in order to belong to his master at every moment. Let not, however, these souls be distressed by their helplessness: it is already a great deal to be able to give oneself over completely into the hands of an almighty Master capable of performing the greatest things by means of the weakest instruments, if they do not resist him.

Let us then without anxiety suffer the outer shell of our life to humiliate us in our own eyes and those of others, or rather let us hide ourselves under this shell and enjoy God who alone is all our good. Let us make profit of this infirmity, of our needs of our necessities in the matter of food and comforts, of our failures, of the contempt of others, of our fears, doubts, troubles and the rest, so as to find all our good in the enjoyment of God who by these things gives himself entirely to us as our sole good.

God wishes to dwell in us in poverty and without all those accessories of sanctity which cause souls to be admired: it is because he wishes to be alone the food of our hearts, the sole object of our complacency. We are so weak that if the splendour of austerity, zeal, almsgiving or poverty were to shine out in us, it would become a part of our joy. But in our way there is nothing but what is disagreeable, and by this means God is the whole of our sanctification, the whole of our support, while the world can only despise us and leave us to enjoy our treasure in peace.

God wishes to be the principle of the whole of our sanctity, and for that reason all that depends on us and our active fidelity is very trifling and in appearance the opposite of sanctity. There can be nothing great in us in the eyes of God except by the way of passivity. Let us then think no more about our sanctity but leave the care of it to God who knows the means to produce it. These all depend on a special protection and operation of Providence; they usually occur unknown to us and through those very things which we dislike most and expect least. Let us walk peacefully in the small duties of our active fidelity without aspiring to great ones, for God will not give himself to us for the sake of any trouble that we can take in the matter. We will be saints of God, of his grace and of his special Providence. He knows the rank he wishes to give us, let us leave it to him to do as he pleases, and without forming henceforward false ideas and vain systems of sanctity, let us be content to love him without ceasing, walking with simplicity in the road which he has traced for us where everything is so little in our eyes and those of the world.

§4. *Fourth trial of souls in the state of self-abandonment: The obscurity of their state and its apparent opposition to the will of God*

But a much more distressing trial for a soul who desires nothing but to love God is the impossibility of feeling sure that it loves him. Formerly by the ideas it formed and the lights it received, it saw what made up the plan of its perfection; but now no longer so. Perfection is given to it contrary to all its ideas and lights and feelings, by all the crosses sent by Providence, by the actions demanded by the duty of the moment, by various inclinations which have nothing good in them except that they do not lead to sin, but which seem far distant from the sublime and extraordinary splendour of virtue.

God hidden in his veils gives himself with his grace in an altogether unknown way, for the soul feels nothing but feebleness under its crosses, disgust with its obligations, while its attractions are only to very commonplace exercises. The idea which it has formed of sanctity reproaches it internally with these low and contemptible dispositions. All the saints' lives condemn it. It knows nothing with which to defend itself; it has light to see a sanctity which, however, brings it desolation, for it has no strength to rise to it, and it does not recognize its weakness as divine order, but as its own cowardice. All the people it knows distinguished by the splendour of their virtues or the sublimity of their speculations look at it with contempt. What an odd saint, they say. And the soul believing them and confused by so many useless efforts that it has made to rise from this degradation is surfeited with obloquy and finds nothing to reply either to itself or others.

It feels itself lost in this dreadful state; it has no support, neither that of the thoughts which used to guide and animate its actions nor that of grace no longer perceptible; but in this loss of everything it finds everything restored, for that very grace that it cannot perceive in, so to say, a new form, gives the soul the hundredfold of what it has taken away, by the purity of its secret effects.

It is no doubt a great blow, like death, to the soul, this loss of the sight of the divine will which retires from its sight to take up a position behind it, as it were, and impels it forward, being no longer its clearly conceived object but becoming its invisible principle.

Experience shows us that nothing so much as this apparent loss inflames the desire of the soul for union with the divine will. What profound sorrow for the soul! . . . No consolation is possible.

To ravish God from a heart longing for nothing but God, what a secret of love! It is indeed a great secret, for by this way and by this way only are pure faith and pure hope established in a soul. Then, indeed, one believes what one does not see and one hopes for what one does not sensibly possess. Oh! how we are perfected by this unknown effect of an action of which we are at once, though invisibly to ourselves, the subject and the instrument. Everything one does seems the fruit of chance and natural inclination. Everything that happens humiliates the soul. When one is really speaking from inspiration, one seems to be speaking from nature. We can never see by what spirit we are moved, the divinest inspiration frightens us, and whatever we may do or feel, we feel incessant contempt for ourselves as if all were faulty. Others are always admired, but we feel miles below them and put to confusion by their every action. We suspect all our lights, we cannot feel sure of any of our thoughts, and we submit, even in excess, to any advice that seems true to us. The divine action seems to keep us far from virtue only to plunge the soul into a profound humility. But this humility does not seem to be such to the soul, it thinks it is suffering from the rigours of pure justice.

The most remarkable thing about this is that in the eyes of those whom God does not enlighten concerning its path, the soul seems animated by quite contrary feelings such as obstinacy, disobedience, contempt and indignation that cannot be cured, and the more the soul tries to reform these disorders, the worse they become, for they are the most proper means to detach it from itself and fit it for divine union.

From this painful trial comes the principal merit of the state of self-abandonment. In the duty of the present moment everything is of a nature to draw the soul away from its path of love and simple obedience. It needs heroic courage and love to stand firm in its simple, active fidelity and sing its part with assurance, while grace sings its own with different melodies and in different keys which do nothing but convince the soul that it is deceived and lost. That is all it hears, and if it has the courage to endure the pealing of the thunder, the flashing of the lightning and the roaring of the tempest and walk firmly in the path of love and obedience to duty and the immediate inspiration given by God, we may say that it resembles the soul of Jesus, and shares the state of his Passion, during which our divine Saviour walked with even step in the path of love for his Father and submission to his will, a path which made him do things in appearance most contrary to the dignity of so holy a soul as his.

The hearts of Jesus and Mary, braving the uproar of this dark night, let the clouds burst asunder and the storm pour down. A deluge of events in appearance most opposed to the designs of God and his commands overwhelm their faculties, but deprived of all support from the senses, they walk on unshaken, on the tiptoe of the heart, so to say, in the path of love and obedience. They fix their eyes solely on what they have to do, and leaving God to act as he pleases in their regard, they endure the whole weight of his divine action. They groan under the burden, but they do not stagger or stop for one single instant. They believe that all will go well, provided the heart keeps to God's path and does not interfere with his action.

§5. *The fruit of these trials. Conduct of a soul undergoing them*

It follows from all that has been said, that in this path of pure faith all that happens in soul and body and the circumstances and events of one's life wears an appearance of death. We should not be surprised at this, for it is precisely the nature of this state. God carries out very successfully his designs on souls under these obscuring veils. Under the name of veils I include misfortune, bodily infirmities and spiritual weakness. All succeeds in the hands of God. He arranges and prepares his highest designs by means of these things so distressing to nature: *Omnia cooperantur in bonum iis qui secundum propositum vocati sunt sancti*. In the shadow of death he produces life, and though the senses are terrified, faith, taking all for the best, is full of courage and assurance.

Since we know that the divine action embraces everything, directs everything, indeed does everything, apart from sin, faith has the duty of adoring, loving and welcoming it in everything. We should do so full of joy and confidence, rising in everything above appearances, the very obscurity of which provokes the triumph of faith. This is the way to honour God and to treat him as God.

To live by faith is then to live in joy, assurance, certitude, confidence in what one must do and suffer at each moment at God's command. It is to animate and sustain this life of faith that God permits the soul to be overwhelmed and carried away on the tumultuous waters of so many pains, troubles, embarrassments, weaknesses and defeats, for faith is needed to find God in all that. The divine life presents itself at every moment in an unknown but very certain manner under such appearances as physical death, damnation in the soul, ruin in temporal affairs. In all this faith finds its nourishment and support. Faith pierces through these appearances and comes to rest on the support of God who keeps it alive. A faithful soul should walk on in confidence, where there is no prospect of sin, taking all these things as the veils of disguise of God, whose intimate presence at once alarms and reassures its faculties.

Indeed, the great God who consoles the humble gives the soul in the midst of its greatest desolation an intimate assurance that it has nothing to fear provided it allows him to act and abandons itself completely to him. In the midst of its affliction at the loss of its Beloved, something tells it that it is in possession of him. It is troubled and upset, and yet in its depths there is a sort of fundamental weight which keeps it unchangeably attached to God.

'Truly,' said Jacob, 'God is in this place and I knew it not.' You are seeking God, dear soul, and he is everywhere, everything cries his name to you, everything gives him to you, he is at your side, around you, within you, and astride your path; he remains with you and you still seek him! . . . Ah, you are seeking the idea of God, while you possess his substance, you are pursuing perfection and it is there all the while in everything that comes to meet you. Your sufferings, your actions, your inclinations are, as it were, the sacramental species under which God gives himself to you, while you are off chasing your sublime ideas. But God will not come to your house clothed in their splendour. Martha tries to please Jesus by good cooking and Magdalen is content to receive him as it pleases him to come to her. He even deceives her and presents himself under the appearance of a gardener when she seeks him according to her own idea of him. The Apostles see Jesus and take him for a phantom.

God then disguises himself to raise the soul to pure

faith, thus teaching it to find him under all sorts of disguises; for once it has learned the secret of God, he may disguise himself as he pleases; it says: 'He is there behind the wall, he is looking through the lattice, he is looking through the windows.' Hide thyself, divine love, try test after test, bind the soul with your attractions and duties, blend, mingle, confuse, break up like spiders' webs all the soul's ideas and standards. Let it lose its foothold and feel no roads or paths nor see any light. After having found thee in solitude and in prayer, in its religious exercises, in sufferings, in services to its neighbour, in the avoidance of society and worldly affairs, and after having tried every known method of pleasing thee, let it no longer be able to find thee in any of these things as heretofore. But grant that the uselessness of its efforts may lead it to abandon them all in order to find thee in thyself, and then in everything, everywhere, without distinction or reflection.

For what an error not to see thee in all that is good, indeed in all creatures! Why seek thee in others than those through which thou wishest to give thyself? Why seek thee under other species than those chosen by thee for thy sacrament? And does not the insignificance of their appearance subserve the merit of our obedience in believing? Dost thou not give fecundity to the root trodden in the earth, and canst thou not render fruitful this darkness in which it is thy will to keep me?

Live on then, little root of my heart, in the hidden bosom of God. Push forth, vitalized by his secret power, the branches, foliage, flowers and fruits which you will be unable to see yourself but which will nourish and rejoice the hearts of others. Give to all who approach you your flowers and your fruit according to their taste rather than your own. May all the slips grafted on you receive an undetermined sap that will only be specified in their own form. Become everything in all souls, in your own be nothing but self-abandonment and indifference.

Dwell then, little silkworm, in the dark and narrow prison of your cocoon until the warmth of grace forms you and hatches you out. Eat all the leaves which grace presents to you and do not regret in the activity of your self-abandonment the peace you have lost. Stop what you are doing when the divine action gives the signal. In your alternating periods of repose and action and your incomprehensible metamorphoses, you must shed your old forms and methods and habits, and in your recurring death and resurrection take on those which the divine action points out to you. Then go on spinning your silk in secret, doing what you can neither feel nor see. Feel throughout your whole being a secret agitation which you will yourself condemn, while you envy your companions in their death-like repose who have not yet reached the point where you are. You still admire them though you have surpassed them. Abandon yourself to this agitation in order to spin a silk in which princes of the Church and the world will be proud to be clothed. After that, what will you become, little worm? . . . What will be the issue for you? . . . What a wonder of grace that a soul can assume so many forms! Who can guess where grace will lead it? Indeed, who could guess the designs of nature on a silkworm, if he had not observed them? All it needs is leaves, that is all. Nature does the rest.

So it is, dear souls, that you cannot know where you come from or where you are going, from what divine idea God's wisdom produced you, or to what end it is bringing you. Nothing remains to you but a completely passive self-abandonment, to let yourself go without deliberation, without following any model or example or method; acting when it is the moment for action, keeping quiet when you should do so, enduring loss when you ought to. In this way, moved by spiritual attraction and self-abandonment, one acts or ceases to act, one reads or not, one puts books and friends on one side, one is silent, one writes, one stops writing without ever knowing what will follow. But after several transformations, the consummated soul receives wings with which to fly up to heaven, leaving on earth a fertile seed to perpetuate its state in other souls.

CHAPTER FOUR

OF THE PATERNAL ASSISTANCE WITH WHICH GOD SURROUNDS THE SOULS WHO ABANDON THEMSELVES TO HIM

§1. *The less the self-abandoned soul feels the support of God, the more efficaciously is he in reality sustaining it*

There is a sort of sanctity in which all the divine communications are luminous and clear. In the passive way of faith, all that God communicates shares his nature and the inaccessible darkness that surrounds his throne: the sentiments the soul feels are confused and cloudy. The soul in this condition, like the prophet, is often afraid of running headlong into snares while crossing this obscure region. Do not be afraid, faithful soul, for this is precisely your path and the way God wishes you to go. Nothing is surer and more infallible than the darkness of faith. But you wish to know what direction to take in such obscurity of faith? Go wherever you like; you cannot lose your way when there is no longer any road to find, all roads being the same in this darkness—you cannot aim at any point, no object is visible. But everything alarms me (says the soul), I seem at each moment to be falling over a precipice. Everything wearies me. I know well enough that I am acting on the principle of self-abandonment, but it seems to me that in everything I can only act by going contrary to virtue. I seem to hear all the virtues complaining that I am abandoning them. The more attractive and pleasing they seem to be, the further the obscure influence under which I act seems to take me from them. I love virtue, but I yield to that obscure impulse; I cannot see that it is leading me aright, but I cannot help believing that it does so. The spirit flies to the light, but the heart is content with darkness. Intellectual people please my mind, but my heart cares only for conversations and sermons in which I understand nothing and my whole state is nothing but an expression of the gift of faith which makes me love and relish principles and truths in which my mind finds neither objects nor ideas, in which it trembles and totters. I know not how, but assurance dwells in the depths of my heart which acts as it is moved, convinced of the goodness of the impression which governs it, not indeed through evidence but through the conviction of faith. And this certitude is victorious over all censures, all fears, all the efforts and ideas of the mind. The spirit may cry out and criticize as much as it likes, the bride feels the presence of the Bridegroom without feeling himself, for when she tries to touch him, he is no longer there. She feels the right hand of the Spouse who is on every side of her, and she would rather stray in self-abandonment to his guidance though it leads her without reason or order, than assure herself of her road by laboriously following the familiar and well-marked paths of virtue. Come then, my soul, let us go to God by the road of self-abandonment; let us confess our inability to produce virtue by our own efforts and industry. But do not let this lack of virtue of our own manufacture diminish in any way our confidence. Our divine guide would not reduce us to the state of being unable to walk, if his divine goodness were not carrying us in his arms. What need have we of lights, assurance, ideas, reflections? What advantage would it be to us, O Lord, to see, to know, to feel, since we are not walking on our feet but are being carried in the bosom of Providence? The darker it grows, the more numerous the chasms, the snares, the fears, the persecutions, the famines, the troubles, the despairs, the purgatories and hells that line our path, the greater shall our faith and confidence be. It is enough to cast our eyes on thee to be safe in the greatest dangers. We will forget all about the road and its condition, good or bad; we will forget ourselves and, completely abandoned to the wisdom, goodness and power of our guide, we will remember nothing but to love thee, to fly not only obvious sin, however slight it may appear, but everything that wears any semblance of sin and to fulfil our ordinary duties. This is the only responsibility, dear Love, that thou leavest to thy children; all the rest is thy affair. The more terrible the rest becomes, the more thy children wait upon and see thy presence; they think of nothing but loving thee without bothering about the rest, and they go on fulfilling their little duties like a child in his mother's arms absorbed in his play as if there were nothing in the world but his mother and his games. The soul must pass beyond all this shadow; the night is not the time for action but for repose. The light of its reason can only augment the darkness of faith: the ray which will pierce it must come from the same height from which that darkness proceeds.

God communicates himself to the soul in this state as *life*, but he no longer presents himself to its vision as the *way* and the *truth*. The bride seeks the Bridegroom in the night: but he is behind her, he holds her in his hands, he moves her in front of him. He is no longer there as object and idea, but as principle and source. There are in the divine action marvellous, unknown and secret sources of inspiration sufficient to deal with all the needs, embarrassments, troubles, upsets, persecutions, incertitudes and doubts of souls who have no longer confidence in their own actions. The more complicated the play, the more delight we anticipate in the *dènouement*. The heart says: All will go well, God has the work in hand; there is nothing to frighten us.

Fear itself, the suspension of the faculties and desolation are the stanzas of this canticle of darkness. It is our joy to omit no syllable of them. We know that all ends with *Gloria Patri*. So each one follows the path of his own wanderings, the very darkness serves for his direction, and doubts do but imply assurance. The more trouble Isaac has to find a victim for the sacrifice, the more completely Abraham places his lot in the hands of Providence.

§2. *The desolation with which God afflicts such a soul is but a loving artifice which will one day make it rejoice*

Souls who walk in light sing the hymns of light, those who walk in darkness, the hymns of darkness. They must both be left to sing to the end the part and the motet which God allots to each. Nothing must be added to what he has made complete; and every drop of this divine bitterness must be allowed to flow, even when it overwhelms and intoxicates the singers. Thus did Jeremias and Ezechiel act; their only words were sighs and sobs and their only consolation was in the continuation of their lamentations. If their tears had been wiped away, we should have lost the most beautiful passages in Scripture. The Spirit who makes them desolate is the only one that can console them; these different waters spring from the same source.

When God appears to be angry, the soul trembles, when he threatens it, it is afraid; there is nothing to be done but allow the divine operation to develop; in its full expansion it brings both the illness and the remedy. Weep and tremble, dear souls, agonize in your anxiety, do not make efforts to get rid of these divine terrors, these heavenly groanings. Receive in the depths of your being these streams from the ocean of suffering which God carried in his holy soul. Go on your way, casting your seed of tears as long as the influence of grace makes them fall; that same influence of grace will dry them unbeknown to you. The clouds will be dissipated, the sun will shine, the spring will cover you with its flowers and the full course of your self-abandonment will reveal to you the admirable variety of the divine action when it is seen in its full extent.

It is truly in vain that man troubles himself, all that happens to him is, as it were, a dream. The shadows in passing efface each other. Afflicting and consoling imaginations follow each other in the sleeper's mind. The soul is the plaything of these appearances which devour each other, and the moment of awakening shows their lack of anything substantial enough to arrest the soul's attention. That moment dissipates all these impressions and one takes no heed either of the dangers or the joys of sleep.

Lord, may I not likewise say that thou holdest asleep on thy bosom all thy children during the night of faith, that thou takest pleasure in causing an infinite number of infinitely various sentiments to pass through their souls, sentiments which at bottom are but holy and mysterious dreamings? In the state in which the night and their sleep place them, they experience authentic and painful terrors, anguish and worries which thou wilt dissipate and transform on the day of glory into true and solid joys.

After this moment of awakening, holy souls, restored to themselves and their full liberty of judgement, will never grow weary of admiring the skill, the finesse, the loving inventions and deceptions of the Bridegroom. Then they will understand how impenetrable are his ways, how impossible it was to guess his riddles, to detect him under his disguises or to admit any consolation when he wished to spread fear and alarm in the soul. At that moment of awakening, a Jeremias and a

Daniel will see that those very things which had caused them inconsolable desolation were to God and the angels a subject of joy.

Do not awaken the bride with the clamour of human wit and action, leave her to her groanings and her trembling pursuit of her Spouse. It is true that he deceives her, he is disguised, she is dreaming. But let her sleep. Leave the Bridegroom to work in the beloved soul and reproduce in it those traits which he alone can paint and express; let him develop them to the full. He will awaken it when the time comes. Joseph is making Benjamin weep. Servants of Joseph, do not reveal his secret to his beloved brother! Joseph is deceiving him, his trick will never be found out, Benjamin and his brothers are plunged into irremediable sorrow. It is only a game of Joseph's; his poor brothers see nothing in his action but a woe without remedy; say not a word. He will put everything right; when the time comes, he will awaken them from their sleep himself, and they will admire his wisdom in causing them to see so much misery in what was in truth the most real subject of joy that they have ever had in the world.

§3. *The more God seems to strip the soul in the state of self-abandonment, the more generously is he really giving to it*

Let us proceed further in the knowledge of the divine action and its loving deceptions. What God seems to take away from a soul of goodwill he really gives, as it were, incognito. Never does he allow it to lack anything: he acts like one who at first maintains a friend by gifts of which he is openly the source but who subsequently, in the interest of his friend, appears no longer willing to oblige him, while continuing his assistance at the same rate anonymously. If the friend did not suspect this mysterious ruse of love, he might well feel hurt. What reflections would he not make on the behaviour of his benefactor? But as soon as the mystery began to unveil itself, God knows what sentiments of tender joy, of gratitude and love, of confusion and admiration would arise in his soul. Would he not burn still more with zealous affections for his friend, and would not this trial confirm him in his attachment, fortifying him for the future against similar surprises?

The application of this parable is simple. The more we seem to lose with God, the more we gain; the more he deprives us of the natural, the more he gives of the supernatural. We loved him a little for his gifts; when we no longer see them, we begin to love him for himself only. It is by the apparent subtraction of those sensible gifts that he prepares this great gift for us, the vastest and most precious of all, for it contains all the rest.

Souls who have once totally submitted themselves to God's action should always interpret everything favourably; yes, everything, whether it be the loss of the most excellent directors, or the suspicion which one entertains in spite of oneself for those who put themselves forward more than one wishes. For, in a general way, the guides who run after souls deserve to incur a little suspicion. Those who are truly animated by the Spirit of God do not, as a rule, display so much hurry and self-sufficiency; they do not propose themselves unless they are called in, and even so they always advance with a certain timidity.

Let the soul that has given itself wholly to God go through these trials without fear, let it not allow its liberty to be snatched from it. Provided that it is faithful to the divine action, that action will work marvels in it in spite of all obstacles. God and the soul perform in common a work the success of which, though it depends entirely on the action of the divine workman, can be compromised only by the infidelity of the soul.

When the soul is well, all goes well, for what comes from God, i.e. the share his action takes in the work, corresponds to the precise degree of the soul's fidelity. God's share is like the upper side of those magnificent pieces of tapestry which are woven point by point from the reverse side. The workman employed on them sees nothing but the point on which he is working and his needle, and these points successively filled make up those magnificent figures which only appear when, at the completion of all the parts, the right side is displayed, although during the time of the work all this marvellous beauty is in obscurity.

So is it with the self-abandoned soul; it sees nothing but God and its duty. The accomplishment of this duty is at each moment but an imperceptible point added to the work, and yet it is with these points that God works his wonders of which we have now and then a presentiment in the time of our pilgrimage, but which will only be known in the great day of eternity.

How full of goodness and wisdom is the conduct of God! He has in such a way reserved to his grace and action alone the sublime, elevated and admirable part of perfection and holiness, and he has so completely left it to our souls to perform with the help of his grace what is small, plain and easy, that there is no one in the world who cannot arrive without difficulty at the most eminent perfection by fulfilling with love lowly and common duties.

§4. *The more God seems to blind the soul in the state of self-abandonment, the more surely is he leading it*

It is principally in the case of those souls who completely abandon themselves to God that the word of St John is fulfilled: *You have no need to be taught, for the divine unction teaches you all things.* To know what God asks of them, they have but to consult this spirit, sound their hearts and listen to what they hear, for the heart is the interpreter of God's will according to circumstances. For the disguised divine action reveals its design not by ideas but by instinct. God's action reveals them to the soul either by the compulsions of necessity preventing it from taking any other line than the one presented, or by an original movement and a sort of supernatural transport which causes the soul to act without reflection, or, again, by communicating to it an inclination or disinclination which, while leaving the soul all its liberty, yet brings it to the point of approaching or avoiding objects. Judging by appearances, a great lack of virtue is shown by this uncertainty. Judging by ordinary rules, there is nothing fixed, uniform or harmonious in this action of God. Nevertheless, fundamentally speaking it is the highest point of virtue to have reached this state, and it is, as a rule, only after long exercise that one attains to it. The virtue of this state is *pure* virtue, perfection itself. The soul that has attained to it is like a musician who combines with a long practice of the art, a perfect theoretical knowledge of music. He is so penetrated by his knowledge that all that he produces has, even unconsciously to himself, the perfection of music, and his compositions, on examination, manifest perfect conformity with the rules of his art. It is evident that his success will never be greater than on those occasions when freeing himself from the rules which, followed too scrupulously, hold genius in bonds, he acts without constraint, and his impromptus, so many masterpieces, will be the admiration of connoisseurs.

So the soul, exercised for years in the science and practice of perfection, forms for itself insensibly, under the influence of those methods and reasonings with which it used to help itself to correspond with grace, a habit of acting in all things by an instinct for God. It seems to it that the best course for it to follow is the first one that presents itself, without the necessity of that string of reasonings that heretofore preceded its decisions. All it can do is to act at random; it can only give itself up to the genius of the grace that cannot but keep it straight. What it does in this state of simplicity is marvellous to enlightened eyes and intelligent minds. It has no rule, yet nothing is more exact than its conduct; no sense of proportion, yet nothing more exquisitely harmonized; it uses no reflections, yet nothing is deeper; it takes no trouble, yet nothing is better arranged; it makes no effort, yet no one is more efficient; it has no foresight, yet in behaviour is always perfectly adapted to every new situation.

Spiritual reading engaged in as the result of divine action frequently has a meaning that never occurred to the author of the book. God makes use of the words and writings of others to convey hidden truth. If it is his will to enlighten us by these means, self-abandoned souls should make use of the opportunity, and any means resulting from divine action has an efficacy always transcending its natural power.

It is characteristic of the state of self-abandonment that, while the soul always leads a mysterious life, it should receive extraordinary and miraculous gifts of God through contact with natural, fortuitous events where nothing is apparent but what is in the normal order of the world and the natural elements. Thus the simplest sermons, the most ordinary conversations and the least remarkable books become for such souls by virtue of the divine design sources of intelligence and wisdom. This is why they gather up with care the crumbs that the self-sufficient man tramples underfoot. All is precious to them, all enriches them. They remain absolutely indifferent to all things, but while they neglect nothing they respect and derive what advantage they can from everything.

Since God is in all things, the use we make of them by his design is not use of creatures but rather enjoyment of the divine action which dispenses its gifts through different channels. These channels do not sanctify by themselves but only as instruments of the divine action which can and frequently does communicate its gifts to simple souls by means of things which appear opposed to the end proposed. In the hands of God, mud is as transparent as light and the instrument he selects is always the unique means to his purpose. Everything is the same to him. Faith believes always that nothing is wanting; the faithful soul does not complain of the lack of means that it may think useful for its advancement, for the Workman who makes use of them supplies by his will for their shortcomings; and this holy will is the whole virtue of creatures.

§5. *The less the soul is capable of defending itself in the state of self-abandonment, the more powerfully does God defend it*

The unique and infallible movement of the divine action always applies the simple soul to the right object at the right time; and it corresponds wisely in everything to God's intimate direction. Sometimes this happens consciously and sometimes unconsciously, the soul being moved by obscure instincts to speech, action or abstention without other motives.

Frequently the determining occasion and reason are only of the natural order; the simple soul sees no mystery here: to it all this is a matter of chance, or necessity, or some convention, nothing at all in its eyes or anyone else's. And yet God's action, which is intelligence, wisdom and counsel for his friends, makes use of all these simple things for their benefit. God, as it were, appropriates them, places them so carefully in the path of those who are planning to harm his friends, that they are unable to achieve their ends.

To deal with a simple soul is in a certain sense to deal with God. What measures can we take against the Almighty whose ways are inscrutable? God takes in hand the cause of the simple soul: it has no need to scrutinize your intrigues, or to match your anxiety with its own in carefully watching all your proceedings; its Bridegroom dispenses it from all these cares: it takes shelter with him and rests on his heart peaceful and secure.

The divine action sets free the soul and delivers it from all those low and feverish methods so necessary to human prudence. All this is necessary for Herod and the Pharisees, but the Magi have only to follow peacefully their star; the child need only rest in the arms of his mother, his enemies do him more good than harm; the more they try to oppose and trap him the more tranquil and free will his activity be. He will do nothing to win them over, he will not pay court to them to escape their blows; their jealousies, suspicions and persecutions are necessary for him. Thus lived Jesus Christ in Judea, thus he still lives in simple souls; he lives in their hearts generous, gentle, free, peaceful, without fear or need of anyone, seeing all creatures in his Father's hands anxious to serve him, some by their criminal passions, some by their holy actions, these by their opposition to him, those by their obedience and submission. The divine action adjusts it all marvellously. There is no lack of anything, there is nothing too much, only just what is needed of both good and evil.

The divine order supplies for the task of each moment the proper instrument, and the simple soul brought up on faith finds everything right and wants neither more nor less than what it has. It blesses on every occasion the divine hand which provides it so perfectly with the means necessary for its task and delivers it from the obstacles to its fulfilment. It accepts its friends and its enemies with equal gentleness, for it was Jesus' way to treat everyone as an instrument in God's hand. We need no one, and yet we also need every one; the divine action renders everything it selects necessary, and everything must be accepted from God's hand, taking everything according to its quality and nature with a certain gentle and humble correspondence, treating the simple simply and the gross with kindness. This was the teaching of St Paul, and what Jesus Christ practised even better.

To grace alone does it belong to give that supernatural stamp to the soul which particularizes and fits itself so appropriately to the nature of each person. This cannot be learned in books, it is a true spirit of prophecy, the effect of an intimate revelation, the teaching of the Holy Ghost. To understand it, the soul must be in the last stage of self-abandonment, in a condition of the most complete detachment from every plan or interest, however holy. The soul must have before its eyes nothing but its one solitary task: to let itself go passively under the influence of the divine action, in order to give itself to what concerns the duties of its state; leaving the Holy Spirit to work in it interiorly without watching what he does, being indeed glad not to know it. Then one is safe, because all that happens in the world exists for no other purpose than the good of souls perfectly submissive to the will of God.

§6. *A soul in the state of self-abandonment, instead of fearing its enemies, finds in them useful auxiliaries*

I am more afraid of my own action and that of my friends than of that of my enemies. No prudence equals that of not resisting one's enemies and of merely opposing to them a state of simple self-abandonment; this is to have the wind at one's back and one can remain at peace. No opposition to the prudence of the flesh is surer than the simplicity which eludes all the traps of worldly wisdom without thinking or even being aware of them. The divine action causes the soul to take such wise measures that it surprises those who are trying to make it stumble. It profits by all their efforts, it rises by means of what is intended to bring it down. Their efforts really bring it to port like galley-slaves rowing at top speed. All the contradictions it meets turn out to its advantage, and by letting its enemies do as they will, it receives from them a service which is continual and so sufficient that its only fear should be lest it mix itself up in the business and take a hand in a work of which God wishes to be the principle, of which his enemies are the instruments and in which it has nothing to do except to watch peacefully what God does and follow with simplicity the inspirations which he gives it. The supernatural producer of the Divine Spirit, the source of these inspirations, strikes infallibly the centre and precise circumstances of every situation, and applies the soul thereto with such exquisite precision that all who oppose it never fail to be broken to pieces.

§7. *A soul in the state of self-abandonment can abstain from saying or doing anything in its own justification: the divine action justifies it*

The large, solid, steady rock on which the self-abandoned soul reposes, safe from waves and tempests, is this design of the divine will continuously present under the veil of crosses and the most ordinary action. God hides his hand in these shadows to sustain and carry those who abandon themselves to him. From the moment that the soul is firmly established in this perfect self-abandonment, it is fully protected against the contradiction of tongues, for it has nothing further to say or do for its own protection. Since the work is of God, its justification must not be sought elsewhere. Its effects and consequences will justify it sufficiently. All that is needed is to allow it to develop. *Dies diei eructat verbum*. One who does not follow his own ideas should not defend himself with words. All our words can do is to express our ideas; where there are no ideas, there should be no words. What end would they serve? To explain our conduct? But the soul is ignorant of the reason for its conduct, which is hidden in the principle causing it to act and of which it has only felt the impression in an ineffable way.

We must then leave to consequences the task of justifying principles. All holds together in this divine chain; each link is firm and solid, and the explanation of the antecedent is found as effect in the consequence. The soul is no longer occupied, fed or sustained by a life of thoughts, imaginations, many words; this is not the strength in which it walks. It sees no longer where it walks or will walk, it no longer helps itself with thought to support the fatigue and inconveniences of the journey; its experience is penetrated by the most intimate sense of its own weakness. The road opens before its feet, it proceeds on it without hesitation.

It is pure, simple and true; it walks in the straight line of God's commandments, gently, leaning on God himself, whom it meets continuously at all the points of that straight line, and the God who is its only quest undertakes himself to manifest his presence in such a way as to avenge it of its unjust detractors.

§8. *God keeps a soul alive in the state of self-abandonment by methods seemingly more adapted to bring it to death*

There is a time when God wishes to be the life of the soul and achieve its perfection himself in a secret and unknown way. When this time comes, all the soul's own ideas, lights, labours, inquiries and reasonings are sources of illusion. And when the soul after several experiences of the sad consequences of its own self-direction at length recognizes its uselessness, it finds that God has hidden and mixed up all the channels of his grace in order to make it find its principle of life in him. Then, convinced of its own nothingness and that all that it can draw from that nothingness is injurious to it, it abandons itself to God so as to have nothing but him. So that God becomes in a sense its life, not through its ideas, illuminations or reflections—all that for it is but a source of illusion—but in his effects and the reality of his graces concealed under the most improbable appearances. The divine operation in itself being unknown to the soul, it receives the virtue and substance of it through thousands of circumstances that to its belief spell its ruin. There is no remedy for this obscurity, we must allow ourselves to be plunged in it. God gives himself in that obscurity and with himself all things in the obscurity of faith; the soul is now but a blind subject, or, if you like, it is as an invalid who, being ignorant of their virtue, experiences only the bitterness of its remedies. The poor patient often thinks that they will kill him; the crises and relapses that follow them seem to justify his fears; nevertheless under this appearance of death he is really gaining health, and he takes them on the word of the doctor who prescribes them.

Thus self-abandoned souls do not bother about their infirmities, except such obvious illnesses as, by their nature, oblige them to stay in bed and take suitable medicaments. The languors and weaknesses of these souls are but illusions and phantasms which they should defy with confidence. God sends them and permits them in order to give exercise to their faith and their self-abandonment, which is the real remedy. Without paying any attention to them, they should bravely pursue their way through the actions and sufferings of God's order, making use of their bodies as hacks whose lives are valueless and serve for any job. So to act is better than to indulge in those delicacies which injure the vigour of the spirit. Such energy of spirit has the power to sustain a feeble body, and a year of a noble and generous life is worth more than a century of care and fears.

We should try to preserve habitually the air and bearing of a child of grace and goodwill. What, after all, have we to fear if we follow the divine fortune? Led, sustained, protracted by it, its children should manifest nothing short of the heroic in their exterior. The terrifying objects which they meet on their way are nothing; these are only designed to embellish their lives with more glorious actions. Their vocation engages them in all sorts of predicaments in which human prudence, unable to see any issue, is made to feel all its weakness and proved to be short-sighted and confounded. It is at this point that the divine fortune appears in all its beauty what in truth it is to all who follow it. It frees them from their troubles more wonderfully than the novelists, aided by their fertile imaginations in the leisure and privacy of their studies, resolve the intrigues and perils of their imaginary heroes who always reach happily the end of their tale. The divine action leads them, by much more admirable devices, through dangers of death and of monsters, of hell and its demons with their snares. God raises these souls to heaven, and makes them the subjects of histories at once real and mystical, more beautiful and strange than any invented by the shallow imaginations of men.

Come then, my soul, let us cross this dangerous territory directed and sustained by the sure, invisible, all-powerful and infallible hand of divine Providence. Let us proceed without fear to the end of our journey in peace and joy: let all that presents itself be matter for our victories. It is to fight and conquer that we march under God's standards: *exivit vincens ut vinceret*. Every step we take under his auspices is a victory, my soul! . . . The Spirit of God has the pen in his hand; he holds his book open in order to continue the unfinished sacred history, the matter of which will only be exhausted at the end of the world.

This history is no other than the account of the actions and designs of God on men. All we have to do so as to figure in this history, is to weave into its web by our union with God's will our sufferings and our actions. Everything that happens to us in the way of action or suffering is not sent us for our loss—no, indeed; it comes to us as the rough material of that Holy Scripture which is growing every day.

§9. *Divine love takes the place of everything else for the souls walking in this way*

While depriving of everything the souls who give themselves absolutely to him, God gives them something that takes the place of all else, whether it be light, wisdom, life or strength; it is his love. Divine love dwells in these souls like a supernatural instinct. Everything in nature has what belongs to its species, every flower has what it needs, every animal follows successfully its instinct, and every creature has its own perfection. Just so is it in the various states of grace: each has its specific gifts, and there is a recompense for each of those whose goodwill fits itself into the state where Providence has placed it.

A soul comes under the divine action as soon as goodwill springs up in its heart, and God's action has more or less influence on it according to the degree of its self-abandonment. The art of self-abandonment is nothing but the art of loving, and divine action is the action of divine love. How can these two loves which seek each other fail to agree when they meet? How could divine love refuse anything to the soul whose every desire it directs? And how could God meet with a refusal from a soul that lives only by him? . . . Love can but ask for what love wishes, and is it possible for love not to desire what it desires?

God pays attention to nothing but a good will. It is not the capacity of the other faculties which attract him, nor their incapacity which repels him. All he demands is a good, pure, upright, simple, submissive, filial and respectful heart. If he finds such a heart, he takes possession of it and of all its faculties and disposes so well all things for its good that it will find materials for its sanctification in everything. If what gives death to others enters the soul, the antidote of its goodwill will not fail to prevent the effects. Should it come to the edge of a precipice, the divine action will steer it away, or prevent it from falling as long as it remains there; should it actually fall, the divine action will raise it up. After all, the faults of such souls are faults of frailty and scarcely perceptible; love can always turn them to their advantage. By his secret inspirations God makes them understand what they are to say or do according to circumstances.

These souls receive in themselves, as it were, flashes of the divine intelligence: *intellectus bonus omnibus facientibus eum.* For the divine intelligence accompanies them in all their steps and withdraws them from the awkward situations in which their simplicity lands them. If they move to some compromising position, Providence arranges some fortunate contacts which repair everything. Multiple intrigues are woven round them, Providence cuts the knots, confounds the authors of these plots and sends on them a spirit of vertigo which causes them to fall into their own snares. Under God's direction, the souls whom it was desired to trap do certain apparently useless things, without thinking, which serve afterwards to deliver them from all the embarrassments into which their own uprightness and the malice of their enemies had thrown them.

Ah! what a fine policy is this goodwill! What prudence in its simplicity, what deliberation in its innocence, and its frankness; what mysteries and secrecy in its uprightness! See young Tobias: he is a mere child, but Raphael is at his side; with such a guide he walks surely; nothing frightens him, he lacks nothing. The very monsters in his path give him nourishment and remedies; the one that attacks him in order to devour him becomes his food. He is occupied with nothing but weddings and banquets, these being, in the order of Providence, his present concern. Not that he has no other affairs, but they are abandoned to the skill of him who has the charge of helping him in everything; they are so well managed that he could never have done so well by himself, for they produce nothing but blessing and prosperity. Yet his mother weeps in utmost bitterness, though his father is full of faith. The child so keenly regretted returns joyfully and enters into the happiness of all his family.

Divine love is, then, for the souls who give themselves wholly to it, the principle of all good. And in order to acquire this inestimable good it is sufficient to will it firmly.

Yes, dear souls, God asks for your heart only; if you are seeking this treasure, this Kingdom in which God reigns alone, you will find it. For if your heart is wholly devoted to God, it forthwith becomes this treasure, this very kingdom that you are desiring and seeking. From the moment that we desire God and his will, we enjoy God and his will, and our enjoyment corresponds to the ardour of our desire. To love God is to desire sincerely to love him; because we love him, we wish to be the instrument of his action, so that his love may exercise itself in and through us.

It is not to the cleverness of the simple and holy that the degree of the divine action corresponds; it corresponds to the purity of its intention and not to the wisdom of the measures it adopts, or the projects that it forms or the means it chooses. The soul may be deceived in these, and it not infrequently happens that it is so deceived, but its upright and good intention never deludes it. Provided that God sees this good disposition, he forgives all the rest, and he accepts as done what it would be certain to do, if sounder views were at the service of its goodwill.

Goodwill has therefore nothing to fear; if it fall it can only fall under that all-powerful hand which guides and sustains it in all its wanderings. It is this divine hand that brings it nearer its goal when it is moving away from it, that replaces it on the road when it wanders off it; in that hand the soul finds its resource when the action of its blind faculties makes it stray; it is the pressure of that hand that makes it feel how completely it should despise them, to count only on God and abandon itself wholly to his infallible direction. The errors into which these good souls fall are then resolved in self-abandonment and never does a good heart find itself at a loss; for it is a dogma of faith that all things co-operate for its good.

§10. *The soul in the state of self-abandonment finds more light and strength in its submission to the divine action than is possessed by the proud souls who resist God*

Of what use are the sublimest lights or divine revelations when one does not love the will of God? That way Lucifer was lost. The course of Providence which God revealed to him in manifesting the mystery of the Incarnation caused him nothing but envy. On the other hand, a simple soul enlightened by faith alone is never wearied of admiring, praising and loving God's order; finding it not only in holy creatures but also in the wildest confusion and disorder. A simple soul is more fully enlightened by a grain of pure faith than Lucifer by all his intelligence.

The knowledge possessed by a soul faithful to its obligations, quietly submissive to the intimate orders of grace, gentle and humble towards all, is worth more than the most profound penetration of mysteries. If only one saw nothing but divine action in all this pride and harshness of human action one would always accept it with humility and respect, and the disorder of creatures would not make us leave the path of order ourselves, how great soever they might be. We should see in them only the divine action which they bear and which they hand on to those who faithfully practise gentleness and humility. We must not look at the path they themselves follow, but walk on firmly in our own, and in this way our gentle pressure will break down cedars and overturn mountains.

What is there among creatures that can resist the force of a faithful, gentle and humble soul? If we would infallibly conquer our enemies we must oppose them with no other arms than fidelity, gentleness and humility. Jesus Christ has put these in our hands for our defence; there is nothing to fear when we know how to use them. We should not be cowardly but generous, for this is the only disposition in which we can use these divine instruments. All that God does is sublime and marvellous and never can individual action at war with God resist one who is united to the divine action by gentleness and humility.

What is Lucifer? He is a brilliant intelligence, the most enlightened of all, but an intelligence discontented with God and his order. The mystery of iniquity is nothing but the result of this discontent manifested in as many ways as possible. Lucifer, as far as lies in his power, wishes to leave nothing in the state in which God has ordained and placed it. Wherever he penetrates, you will always find the work of God disfigured. The more lights, knowledge and general capacity a person has the more he is to be feared, if he has not the foundation of piety which consists in contentment with God and his will. It is the regulation of the heart that places us in union with the divine will; without that union, everything is but pure nature and, usually, pure opposition to the divine order; God has not, properly speaking, any instruments but humble souls: though he is always contradicted by the proud, he does not fail to make them serve, like slaves, the accomplishment of his designs. When I see a soul who makes God and submission to his orders its all, however deficient it may be in other things, I say: There is a soul who has great talents for serving God. The Holy Virgin and St Joseph were like that. The rest, without that, frightens me and I fear to find there the action of Lucifer; I keep on my guard and I fortify myself in my stronghold of simplicity in order to oppose it to the whole of this life of the senses which, by itself, is for me nothing but brittle glass.

§11. *The soul in the state of self-abandonment can see God in the proud soul who fights against his action. All creatures, good or evil, reveal God to it*

The simple soul practises no other devotion than the order of God. It respects this order in the irregular actions which the proud man performs to insult it. The proud man despises a soul in whose eyes he is nothing; for it sees nothing but God in him and his actions. Often he thinks that its humility means that it fears him, although it is but the sign of the loving fear it has of God and his will which it perceives in the proud man.

No, poor fool, the simple soul is not afraid of you. You awaken its compassion. It is to God it is replying when you think it is speaking to you; it looks on you as one of his slaves or rather as a shadow under which he is disguised. So the higher the tone you take, the lower is its answer. All your tricks and acts of violence are for it favours of Providence.

The proud man is an incomprehensible enigma to himself but very intelligible to a simple soul enlightened by faith.

This discovery of the divine action in all that passes within us and around us is the true knowledge of things. It is a continual revelation of things; it is a ceaselessly renewed commerce with God; it is the enjoyment of the Bridegroom, not in secret in the wine-cellar or the vineyard, but openly and in public, without fear of any creature. In its depths, it is peace, joy, love and contentment in God, seen, known (or rather believed) to be living and always working in the most perfect way in everything that happens. It is the eternal paradise which is, indeed, only known and savoured in dark and shapeless forms; but the Spirit of God who is the stage-manager of this life by his continual and fecundating action, will say at the moment of our death: let there be light: *Fiat lux*; and then we shall see the treasures concealed by faith in that abyss of peace and contentment with God who is present at every moment in all we have to do and suffer.

When God gives himself in this way, the ordinary becomes extraordinary, and this is why nothing seems extraordinary. For this path in itself is extraordinary and it is quite unnecessary to adorn it with irrelevant marvels. It is itself a miracle, a revelation, a continuous joy, apart from our trifling venial faults, but it is a miracle which, while it renders marvellous all our everyday life of the senses, has nothing in itself that is marvellous *to* the senses.

§12. *God assures to the souls who are faithful to him a glorious victory over the powers of the world and of hell*

It is in order to augment the merits of faithful souls that the divine action hides itself here below under the appearance of weakness, but its triumph is none the less certain for that.

The history of the world is nothing but the history of the war waged by the powers of the world and of hell since the beginning against the souls humbly devoted to the divine action. In this war, the advantages seem all on the side of pride, and yet humility always wins the day. The figure of this world is presented to us under the image of a statue of gold, bronze, iron and clay. This mystery of iniquity, shown in a dream to Nabuchodonosor, is but a confused assemblage of all the interior and exterior actions of the children of darkness, who are also represented by the Beast that comes out of the bottomless pit to make war from the beginning on the interior and spiritual man; all that happens today is nothing but the continuation of this war. The monsters follow each other, the abyss devours and regurgitates them in incessantly renewed jets of smoke. The battle begun in heaven between Michael and Lucifer is still going on. The heart of that proud and envious angel has become an inexhaustible abyss of all sorts of evils. He caused the revolt of the angels in heaven; and his entire occupation since the creation of the world is to keep constantly renewed the supply of evil men who take the place of those swallowed by the abyss. Lucifer is the leader of those who will not obey the Almighty. This mystery of iniquity is the inversion of the order of God; it is the order or rather the disorder of the devil. This disorder is a mystery, for it conceals under beautiful appearances irremediable evils. All the evil men from Cain to those who ravage the world today have had the appearance of great and powerful princes who have produced a great effect in the world and whom men have worshipped. This appearance of pomp is also a mystery; in reality these princes are the beasts who have come up out of the abyss, one after the other, to overturn God's order. This order (which is another mystery) has always opposed to them truly great and powerful men who have slain these monsters, and as hell vomits forth new ones, heaven has brought to birth its heroes who have combated them. Ancient history, sacred and profane, is nothing but the history of this war. The order of God has always remained victorious; those who have been on his side have triumphed with him and are happy for eternity; injustice has never been able to protect the deserters, but has paid them with death, and that an eternal death!

The man who has wickedness in his mind always believes himself invincible. But, O God! how can we resist thee? A single soul with hell and the world against it can fear nothing if it be on the side of self-abandonment to God's order. This monstrous show of impiety armed with so much power, this golden head, this body of silver, bronze and iron is but a phantom of iridescent dust. A tiny pebble scatters it to the winds.

How admirable is the Holy Spirit in this dramatic representation of all the ages! So many revolutions which create such havoc among men, such heroes who come in such splendour like so many constellations moving in the sky over our heads; so many wonderful events—all this is but a dream which Nabuchodonosor forgets when he wakes, however terrible the impression it has made on his mind.

All these monsters come into the world only to exercise the courage of the children of God, and when these have learned enough, God rewards them with the pleasure of killing the monster, and calls new athletes to the arena. And so this life is a continual spectacle which is the joy of heaven, the training of the saints on earth and the confusion of hell.

Thus, all that is opposed to God's order does but result in making it more adorable. All who freely serve iniquity become the slaves of justice, and the divine action builds the Heavenly Jerusalem with the ruins of Babylon.